A PEOPLE'S PRACTICE

A People's Practice

A Paper Chase Compendium

Gary Green

Moix Publishing Company, LLC
1001 La Harpe Boulevard
Little Rock, Arkansas 72201
www.moixpublishing.com

First edition: August 2021
ISBN: 978-1-7337964-5-3

Cover and book illustrations: Nathaniel Dailey

Cover and book design: H. K. Stewart

Printed in the United States of America

This book is printed on archival-quality paper that meets requirements of the American National Standard for Information Sciences, Permanence of Paper, Printed Library Materials, ANSI Z39.48-1984.

To **young lawyers**,
who make me smile, much like we all smile
when we see young parents with children
who remind us of those golden times gone by.
To the lawyers' lawyers we each strive to be.
And to that part of heaven
that is always in the present tense.

Contents

ACKNOWLEDGMENTS

I cannot tell you how many drafts there were, but Tara Ashton could, as she cheerily assisted with every one. Daughter Kayce and wife Patricia comprised a focus group. Renae and Michael Oldner traded services for help with the flow. Nathaniel Dailey gave additional perspective by redrawing the courthouses, and H.K. Stewart brought it all together.

Gary Green

A People's Practice

1. WHY?

I always thought I would write a book when I retired, but, the good Lord willing and the creek don't rise, that will never happen. That will never happen as long as I have my life and health, because I love practicing law.

I love everything about it. Interacting with people, helping them, helping fellow lawyers, providing for my family, doing something positive for my community.

I love the creative force it gives me, the entrepreneurial spirit that goes with a law firm.

I love the competition—with like-minded lawyers for the clients we might get to know as friends, and with opposing counsel as we each respect the adversarial system.

I love the complexity of the law.

I love the reasonable risk that is required to be a good trial lawyer.

I love that things at the law office change all the time. It never gets boring.

I love the trials. I love it when the trial is over, the jury is out, and I am just waiting on the verdict. That's when you really get to know opposing counsel, the judge, and your client.

I love it when I learn new things about the law, and I love it when I am able to share some things I have learned from others. That is why I am writing this paper chase compendium. The way I look at it, if I learn one new thing at a continuing legal education seminar, it was worth it. My hope is that you learn one new tidbit from reading this, and that you smile or scratch your head at the other stuff.

Early on I had the occasion to call on a doctor who, through the introduction of a doctor friend of mine, had agreed to discuss with me a potential medical negligence claim. I cannot now remember if I started or ended my spiel with the comment, "I think I have got a case," but it earned me a quick rebuke from the wise doctor: "First of all, if you want me to help, you must understand I am offended by a lawyer who puts himself first. If you tell me you are trying to help a client, I will try to help you. You do not have a case; you have a client who needs help. Don't forget that." I was embarrassed, but it was one of the best lessons I have learned.

It should be a lawyer's Golden Rule, to put the client first. To always communicate in such a way that others sense that you put your client first and, thus, to help you help your client.

I. Persuasion

If you use any rule of persuasion, use this one.

There are many rhetorical devices that help us speak for our clients, but I have found the rule of three to be the most effective, ingenious, and persuasive.

We learn in law school to "think like a lawyer." Remember IRAC? Issue, reasoning, analysis, conclusion. Why have we shortened that four step process to a three step process ("Issue, reasoning, conclusion"; or "facts, issue, conclusion")? IRAC was a catchy mnemonic device, but not a good example of how we remember.

The brain tends to remember in groups of three. And complex problems sometimes can be tackled better when we think in terms of three. Understand and harness this concept to improve almost everything you do, personally and professionally.

Churchill quotes are good to help understand.

> *"We shall defend our island, whatever the cost may be, we shall fight on the beaches, we shall fight on the landing grounds, we shall fight in the fields and in the streets, we shall fight in the hills; we shall never surrender."*
>
> — Winston Churchill

Usually people remember, "We'll fight them in the air, on the beaches, and in the streets."

> *"I have nothing to offer but blood, toil, tears and sweat."*
>
> — Winston Churchill

History has shortened this to, "blood, sweat, and tears."

Ah, the power of three. The rule of three. We use it unconsciously. Why not consciously put it to work for us to better help us organize, remember, and speak? To help us persuade? If it is easier for us to remember in groups of three, why not deliver in the same way?

How have I personally used the Power of Three to improve my performance? Many, many, many ways. Here is the most important way for me:

Never use notes at the podium again. Every speech, prayer, or argument should be jelled down into its three most important components. Memorize the three components. Now go to the podium. It goes without saying you will organize the three into beginning, middle, and end. And it goes without saying that the three most important parts for almost anything are preparation, preparation, preparation.

Why not boil down the most important questions for your next witness to three? Or organize into three easily remembered points your opening statement, closing argument, or rebuttal?

What are the three most important things you need to get done today? What are your three most important cases? The three least worthy—(which perhaps should be closed)?

Keep it simple—what are the three most important points?

It is fun to think about how powerful this concept is. Was Johnny Cochran using power of three when he implored, "If the Glove doesn't Fit, you must Acquit"?

The Rule of Three is a topic deserving of volumes, and, in case you haven't noticed, I am limiting topics to a page or two. Do yourself a favor and follow through.

Tell me, and I will forget. Show me, and I might remember. Involve me, and I will learn, said Ben Franklin.

No pressure, but you've got to make them cry to get a good plaintiff's verdict.

You will need to use every rhetorical device you can muster. What follows is not an exhaustive list. Using rhyme, rhythm, and repetition are so obvious they need not be mentioned. "First and last" becomes obvious when we realize we tend to remember what we hear first and what we hear last. Others, such as theme, the power of three, and embedded commands, deserve mention unto themselves.

Every case should be represented by a theme, preferably one sentence that encapsulates the big picture. Themes emerge from working the case and from paying attention. Did, "If the glove doesn't fit…" emerge as a theme?

Country songs are a good source for themes. A couple I have used with good results are Jason Isbell's "Something More Than Free"—("Sunday morning I'm too tired to go to church, but I thank God for the work"); and Brothers Osborne's, "It Ain't My Fault."

Themes can be mentioned often, or only once. (Beware mentioning too early so as not to draw a cross theme).

Themes can be anchored. Consider standing in the same place, or touching the same something, e.g., your glasses, each time you mention the theme.

Remember again the theme, "If the glove doesn't fit"? In addition to the rule of three and rhyme, do you detect the embedded command, the "…if, then…"?

If we hear a premise, followed by a call to action, our mind's eye links the two as a logical action.

If you find the Defendant was negligent and that the negligence was the proximate cause of Plaintiff's damages, then your verdict must be for the Plaintiff.

If _____, then _____.

Framing refers to how we look at something, how we present it, how we frame it.

Do we crop part of the big picture to draw the eye to what is important? Do we use the wide angle or the telephoto lens?

Framing refers to different ways of presenting the same evidence to evoke different emotions, perceptions, and reactions. If I live in the U.S., a country of 328,000,000 people, and, per blood tests, there is a 98% chance I am the father of little Johnny, it sounds like I am positively the father of little Johnny—until you consider 3,280,000 other males in the U.S. might be the father. Be careful how you word (frame) something.

Use similes, metaphors, and stories to help explain.

Causation is a concept that can be difficult for a lay person to understand, particularly in a medical negligence case.

Tell the story of the doctor who ran the red light (negligent) but hit no one and did not cause anyone else to wreck, so no causation; no harm, no foul.

The story of the three legged milk stool I learned from a wise Texas lawyer. If you'll recall an old milk stool, it had three legs. Knock any one of the legs off, and the stool would fall. A case is like a three legged milk stool. The three legs are liability, causation, and damages. If any one of these elements is lacking, the case fails. I use this story to explain to potential clients why I cannot help them.

Use the story of the police officer who shot the injured horse to underscore how sometimes we might not complain, even when we are really hurt.

1968. First day of high school basketball practice. One teammate was late getting dressed out. Once all of us finally were on the court getting warmed up, the coach walked to the center of the court and without any explanation ordered us to the far end of the court where we started our sprints to the opposite end. We sprinted back and forth until nobody needed anymore warming up. Then we ran "the lines." To the free throw line, and back; to the half court line, and back; to the far free throw line, and back; to the far out of bounds line, and back. Then we ran the lines some more. Next we ran laps around the court. Too many. We were tired. Next we "ran the stands." Up and down, up and down, two summits on one side of the stands; then down the stairs and across the court to the other side for two summits there. We ran the stands until we were holding our sides, afraid to stop but stopping, heaving to breathe. The coach walked back to the center of the court and summoned us all there. "Gentlemen, there are two lessons you must learn before we start practice. When one of you lets down the team, the whole team suffers. And it is better to be an hour early than a minute late."

Fetal monitoring strips. Variable decels. HIE. Not too many years ago it all would have been Greek to me. But we were representing a child. A severely injured child. A child whose parents could not speak English. We lawyers had to understand the medicine and then find a way to teach the medicine to the jury. And we had to do what we could to have the jury receptive to helping someone who did not speak English.

The baby was born by C-section at 3:40 p.m.

All experts agreed that had she been delivered 30 to 40 minutes earlier, there would have been no injury.

The doctor had visited the mom, a multiparous patient, at the hospital that morning—at 9:30 a.m.—and had not seen her again until she was called over for the STAT delivery.

All agreed that the second stage of labor began no later than noon. The doctor did not lay hands on the patient for more than three hours after the start of the second stage of labor.

On the Friday afternoon of the second week of trial, we found ourselves at the local pizzeria, going over the trial and the tribulations presented. We needed a good team analogy. The doctor and the nurse were supposed to be working together as a team. They testified they always had worked as a team in the past; that they respected each other. But they had not worked together this time; had not communicated well. According to the doctor, the nurse had not communicated at all; according to the nurse, the doctor had not listened. Long before the start of the trial I knew I was going to use "better to be an hour early than a minute late," but until the mention of the team analogy I had not thought to include the story about the teammate who was late for practice. As I told the trial team the story at the pizzeria, we all knew it made for a good theme.

Our theme was only spoken once, in closing rebuttal. It was never mentioned before then. No chance was given to the defense to attack or cross-theme. There was no hint to the defense that they should stress even more that the nurse is the "eyes and ears of the doctor"; that the doctor should not be required to be at the hospital until "the baby's ears were sticking out." There was no telegraphing our complete reliance on our own OB-GYN expert that the doctor had an independent duty.

In rebuttal the jury was reminded of the doctor's independent duty to find out what was taking so long to deliver the child; of the parents' tried and true duty and promise to take care of their child for the rest of their lives; of the jurors' duty to follow the law; and of the duty of the attorney to represent this child, a duty I was then taking off of my shoulders and placing onto the shoulders of the jury, reminding them, "You're the coach now. Teach the doctor it is better to be an hour early than a minute late."

On day one of trial, during voir dire, I had asked the panel to complete the missing word from red, yellow, black and _____. When three or four jurors answered "white" at the same time, I knew we would have a good jury; that the jury members would know from their days of Sunday school that the law must be color blind.

On the penultimate day of trial, closing arguments ended in the early afternoon. The jury deliberated until 5:00 p.m. and then asked to be excused until the following morning. Each day trial had begun at 8:30 a.m. The main courthouse doors remained locked until 8:00 a.m., but a basement door could be accessed earlier. That final morning I stopped for breakfast and checked emails. I knew I had to be early again, and I was. (Fifty years later I'm still more likely to be early than late. Somehow I can't help it.) I strode up to the main door of the courthouse to find it still locked. As I turned to head for the basement door I couldn't help but notice four jurors sitting in their parked cars, almost an hour early, waiting for the courthouse doors to open. I knew it was going to be a good day.

For me, telling a story is taking something I know to be true and telling it in such a way they will listen. Telling a story is not telling a lie.

Telling a story is telling a truth in a way it can be received by others.

What is a good warning?

Is "Stop!" a good warning?

Some might say "Stop!" is a perfectly good warning, but it is not. Simple is good, but not too simple. A good warning not only calls attention to danger, but also warns of the consequences of not heeding the warning.

How about, "Stop, or I'll shoot!" Now that's a good warning.

Those with superior knowledge have a duty to warn of danger. Cases should be screened with this in mind. Duty to warn issues are commonly associated with product liability cases, but I have used the question of "What is a good warning?" in medical negligence cases, and screen all personal injury cases for warning issues.

Tell them the why. My next office will be in a downtown warehouse that I now share with my stepdaughter. She or her mother often works there when no one else is around. I usually cruise by the place on weekends just to check on things. Recently a hobo was sleeping on the dock, near the entryway to the building. "Sorry, sir, but you can't stay here."

"Oh yea. What are you gonna do about it?"

"I could call the police, but I don't want to do that. Several people work here, and they'd be frightened to find you blocking their entrance to the building."

"I understand. I'm leaving."

From a legal and not a religious perspective, what's the first thing you think about when you consider the golden rule? If this were a psychological test and you were asked to utter the first word that came to your mind, what would that word be? Would it be, "Objection"? Mistrial"? "Improper"?

Most lawyers wouldn't say, "persuasion," but the golden rule is argument so persuasive that it can get you reversed, usually during summation, at the end of a long, difficult, and expensive trial.

A "golden rule" argument is any argument that asks the jurors to consider what they would want or do if they or a member of their family were a party at the trial. Variants include the request that jurors put themselves in the plaintiff's shoes, that they ask themselves what damages they would want their child or spouse to receive in such circumstances, or that they ask themselves what sum they would accept in exchange for having to endure the plaintiff's injuries.

The underlying reason that a golden rule argument is improper is because what a juror would think or do is not relevant. It is the reasonable person standard that is relevant.

This does not mean that every argument that approaches a golden rule argument should be avoided.

1. Don't say, "Put yourself in the Plaintiff's shoes/place.

2. Be creative. Set up your near golden rule arguments in voir dire.

3. Do ask in voir dire, "Whom do you look up to, respect?" (Then indirectly reference that relationship in closing arguments).

4. But be careful with later arguments that ask the jurors to, "Imagine yourself or someone you care about in the place of ..."

5. Avoid the trigger words *you, yourselves,* etc. when making comparisons—they might not get you reversed, but, at a minimum, they invite objections/interruption of your cadence/persuasiveness.

6. With the above admonitions in mind, do use second person when you speak to a jury. Save third person for formal writing.

I learned about the bystander effect from a Phillip Martin article in the newspaper. In a nut shell, a study was performed establishing that when a group is shown a choking person, no one tends to act. (They all wait for the other person to do it). But show the same to an individual, and the individual rushes to administer a Heimlich maneuver. Imagine using that in your next rebuttal.

I've used the story of the eggshell plaintiff in closing argument, followed by the story of bystander effect, to demonstrably motivate a jury into action. Our client suffered from serious pre-existing conditions that were hammered by the defense. Of course those pre-existing conditions had nothing to do with the Defendant's negligence. I argued those specific pre-existing conditions as the reasons the Defendant gave the farmer for not paying for the eggs.

"If she hadn't had diabetes she wouldn't have been affected by the loss of a kidney; If she hadn't had peripheral artery disease, she wouldn't have been so affected by the loss of a kidney; If she hadn't had COPD, she wouldn't have been so affected by the loss of a kidney; If she had been carrying potatoes rather than those fragile eggs, she wouldn't have been hurt at all."

Then I told the story of bystander effect, substituting our client as the choking person.

When I rhetorically asked that one of the jurors please stand up and deliver the Heimlich maneuver, a police officer (who turned out to be the jury foreman) literally flinched as he started to get up from his chair.

Send messages to one person, copy everyone else involved. (If you send the same message to several people all at once, they'll all tend to ignore it, thinking someone else will handle it).

12. ILLUSIONS OF REMEMBERING

Ever witnessed a police line-up? Ever cross examined an eye witness who previously had picked someone from a line-up? Did you ask them whether the police had shown a photo of the defendant before the line-up? Whether photos of other people in the line-up had been shown? How long was spent viewing the subject at the original scene, at the photo line-up, at the actual in-person police line-up? Whether there was a familiarity with the person picked from the line-up because of the photograph? Whether the person just identified in court was remembered from the scene, the photo line-up, or the actual line-up? Whether the person identified in court is an illusion of familiarity?

A good voir dire question to assist in later argument: "Have you ever seen someone on the street, thought you knew them, maybe even waved, only to realize you had mistaken the person for someone else?"

13. INTENSITY MATCHING

This one I got from Daniel Kahneman's *Thinking, Fast and Slow*, which I guarantee, if you'll read cover to cover, you'll come up with at least ten good ideas for your next jury trial.

"In classic experiments, people adjusted the loudness of a sound to the severity of crimes; other people adjusted loudness to the severity of legal punishments. If you heard two notes, one for the crime and one for the punishment, you would feel a sense of injustice if one tone was much louder than the other."

No wonder the Liberty Bell cracked.

Imagine a Justice Bell...

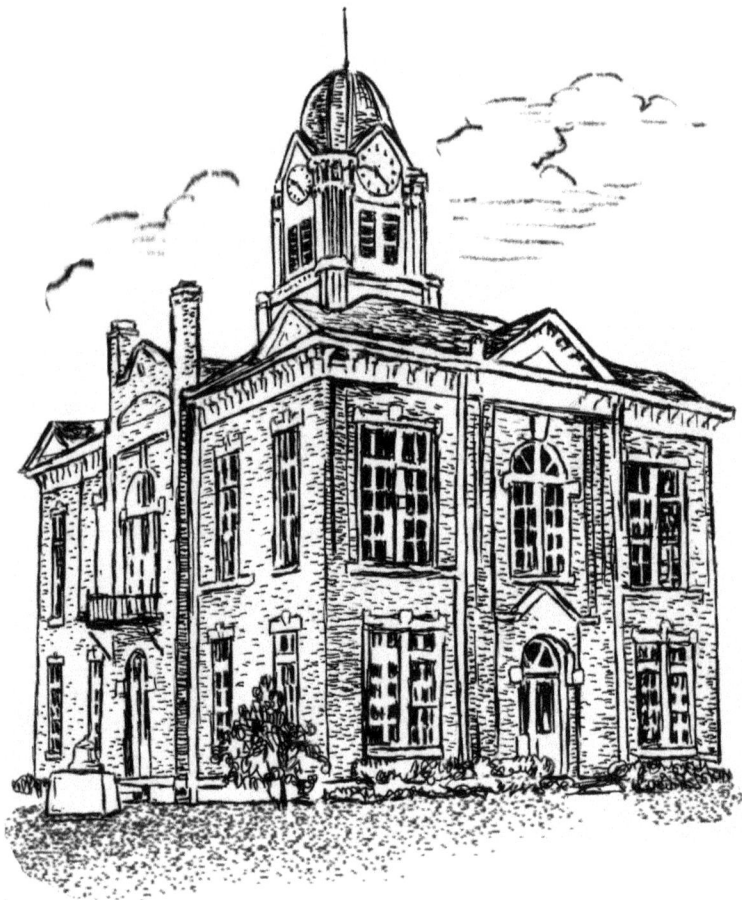

II. LITIGATION

14. LITIGATION

After a grade crossing wrongful death trial in Texarkana I was exhausted. I'd driven back to Little Rock after the defense verdict, thinking about the gruesome photographs of my client's body eviscerated on the tracks. (It was before David Hodges' Franklin v. Healthsource—the family had turned down a settlement offer, partly because of a workers' compensation lien.)

I went to bed, lying on my back, and immediately fell asleep.

In the middle of the night I was awakened by the feel of a cold, hairy, grisly arm on my throat. I grabbed it with my right hand, eerily cold to the touch, and jumped out of bed in order to fling it like a discus through the plate glass window.

In the third step of the discus throw I realized I had grabbed my left arm (which had fallen asleep and was cold to the touch, insensitive, and heavy on my throat) and was about to fling it and myself with it through the glass. I was single at the time and happy there had been no one there to see me.

I thought we'd done everything right. We sued the engineer as well as the company so as to keep the case in state court. Called all the right experts.

But nothing worked, not even the rhetorical questions to the engineer, "Had you braked as soon as you saw the vehicle, isn't it true you were speeding so fast you couldn't have stopped in time?" and "Isn't it true that engineers hate to sound the warning whistles because it's such a deafening sound inside the locomotive?"

It always hurts to lose a trial, but this one especially so because a friend had called on me to help the widow, and I didn't deliver.

It hurt even more when I heard a week or so later the disgusting celebration the defense lawyers had at one of the local watering holes, loudly boasting the verdict and mocking the widow's appearance, demeanor, and plight.

Litigation is not for the faint hearted.

It's an endurance test.

Litigation requires lots of resources. Lots of time.

It's stressful.

Plaintiff's personal life, including medical and social histories become public record.

But, ideally, it can change your client's world for the better.

15. Mock Jury/Focus Groups

E very lawyer who has ever tried a serious case has used a focus group. That focus group might have been a jury of one and compromised of the lawyer's spouse or a family member or friend, but we cajoled someone into listening to us test what we were planning to present at the real upcoming trial.

I once paid a lot of money to a trial psychologist to conduct a focus group. The psychologist prepared a narrative explanation of the facts and law and then presented the narrative along with a "verdict form" to forty people chosen to match as closely as possible the anticipated jury pool of the case on which we were working. To assist in evaluating the damages, of the forty verdict forms, the psychologist discarded the two highest and the two lowest. I was surprised by the high amount of the average, which was presented to the defense attorney in written form and helped to settle the case. But what surprised me more and has continued to surprise me with every mock jury or focus group since, were the questions, observations, or suggestions made by the focus group participants. The input is invaluable. Focus groups, mock jurors, and actual jurors usually do not take the same path to resolve a case that the attorneys think they will.

By the way, since hiring the psychologist to assist with my first focus group, I have since conducted them myself, drafting the narrative and asking friends and acquaintances to complete the questionnaire/verdict form.

A mock jury was consulted in a recent trial regarding a drunken trucker. We were of the opinion before questioning the mock jurors that anyone who worked in the trucking industry would not be a good juror for us. Just the opposite proved to be true. People who worked for the trucking companies knew the rules regarding trucking compliance and supervision. They were incensed the drunk trucker was on the road in the first place, knew he reflected badly on their occupation, and would have awarded damages higher than most.

Focus groups and mock juries make you prepare; they make you practice the presentation of the case. Focus groups are indispensable. Costs permitting, mock juries are invaluable.

Many lawyers and most law professors will tell you to avoid the professional expert witness. The reasoning goes that the jury will not appreciate someone who has testified hundreds of times, particularly when it is testimony that usually is in favor of a particular side, either Plaintiff or Defendant. I have tried it both ways, and my experience is that I would rather have a credible expert who has been ridden hard and put up wet than an expert who is not litigation savvy. Too many times a presumably non-litigation savvy expert has dropped the ball because she does not understand the legal lingo, the standard of care, or the fact that litigation can be so downright confrontational, antagonistic, and adversarial.

I know it is our job as trial lawyers to educate the novice expert, but my experience is that they do not listen well.

I want an expert who is going to teach me something about the case.

I want an expert who is going to teach me how to better handle the case as a lawyer.

I want an expert who is tried and true, is constantly on the lookout for the trick question, and is unflappable.

Although the other side will call him a whore no matter what, I want an expert who will not overstate anything about the case, but also who will not let the other side put words in his mouth.

Seek out an expert based upon reputation. Listservs are invaluable, as are university faculties. But probably the best source is the friend of a friend referral. E.g., when you have located the perfect pediatric neurologist for that birth injury case you are working on, ask her if she will introduce you to her friend over in the radiology department for that neuroradiology expert you are going to need.

Might as well find the best. I'd rather defend a frequent flyer than one who can't carry and defend his weight.

17. Mediation

Mediation is good when a client has unreasonable expectations. Mediation can help get resolved a claim that should not go to trial. Mediation is a good tool for use in the small case that does not justify the expense of trial.

As a general rule, it never hurts to mediate; but do not let the other side conduct more discovery during the mediation than they allow to be conducted of them. For this reason, have agreements on the front end regarding who will appear at the mediation and that they will have plenary authority.

I generally do not take my clients to mediation unless the economically responsible defendant or insurance company representatives are going to be present.

In cases where damages are great and liability is clear, mediation can be used to get reserves set higher for further negotiations down the road, or to communicate the seriousness of the case and your client's willingness and readiness to go to trial. When big dollars are at stake, insurance companies usually do not authorize as much for settlement at a mediation as they later will authorize immediately prior to or after the beginning of trial.

When choosing a mediator, it usually doesn't matter which one is chosen. Let the other side choose. Have or develop a history with that mediator that shows you will try the right case; that you will settle the ones that should be settled.

At one mediation, the mediator's proposal was for recovery of $350,000. The case went to trial where a two million dollar verdict was entered. Later at a second mediation the case settled for close to the verdict amount. The same mediator was called upon the second time around because he was respected by the defense and known to be smart. I knew that he knew that once a verdict had been entered value had been set. At the second mediation we were just adjusting the value to recognize the risk of appeal.

It does not hurt to compliment those in attendance at the mediation on the hard work done in getting to the point of being able to evaluate the case and the good faith of agreeing to participate. While it can be difficult to transition from litigation mode to settlement mode, your opening remarks at the mediation can help with the transition.

Never leave a mediation before the "final offer."

I am not a fan of court ordered mediations, because, in my experience, both parties have to want to try to mediate to maybe make it successful. If you do have to deal with a court ordered mediation be sure to keep a written record of your attempts to comply with the order.

I recall one mediation of a TBI trucking case. Our demand was higher than what the insurance company wanted to pay. I had stepped into the men's room and was washing my hands when the adjuster strode in, walked over to the urinal and, while looking over his shoulder, extremely vehemently growled, "Hey Green, f___ you."

It did not settle that day. They had offered primary policy limits of 1 million prior to the mediation. I believe they came to 1.2 million by the end of the day. A week or two later after getting past a motion for summary judgment, the offer increased to 1.3 million. The following week after the motion in limine was heard, the offer increased to 1.4 million. After the first day of trial it was 1.5 million. After the second day of trial 1.6 million. On the third day, right before the plaintiff was to testify, the adjuster from the men's room, who was not an attorney, called out from the gallery, "Your honor, may we approach the bench?" The judge looked at me and the defense attorneys (who were shaking their heads) and said, "Of course, come on up here, sir. What is it?"

"Judge, we want to settle."

"Mr. Green, why don't you visit with this gentleman and report back. Court is in recess."

I heard in my head Guy Clark's, "Down by the creek where the water goes slow the green back heron and the moccasin know, all things come to him who waits yet he is lost who hesitates."

The case settled for over 5 million.

Am I proud of that? Yes. But I tell the story to underscore how value can go up after mediation.

18. ARBITRATION

Trial lawyers must realize that mediators and arbitrators are hired more often by the insurance companies than by plaintiff lawyers and that loyalties develop because of this. It is extremely rare that a plaintiff's lawyer should agree to arbitrate a case.

If mediation does not go your way, you can walk away and try the case. If arbitration goes against you, it is final.

The cost of mediation/arbitration usually can be negotiated to be borne by the defense.

I once negotiated a high-low arbitration where it was agreed in advance my client would receive a maximum of 3X and a minimum of 1X, regardless of the arbitrator's decision. The arbitrator rendered recovery of X-30%. While my client was quick to collect the approximate value I had placed on the case, the insurance company was happy to pay it, (because their main concern was in limiting their liability); it was obvious to me that the arbitrator awarded an amount of money that would be remembered favorably by the insurance company in the future.

19. YOU'RE NEVER READY TO TRY A CASE

While your attitude should be you're ready to try it tomorrow, there is always something else. A while back I devoted two years to a compelling and worthy case. Family suffered. Our offices suffered. And was I ready on the day of trial? Of course not. I had over prepared in some areas and paid too little attention to others. Information and obstacles continued to stream in even after the start of the trial. We had striven for perfection but could only produce herded chaos, a trial. Early on we made a commitment to go forward, prepared an outline of how to get there, and then followed the outline to conclusion. Certainly it is an oversimplification to describe in one sentence how to try a case, but not to make it that simple keeps a lot of cases from getting tried. Do your best, but do not be a perfectionist to the point of not herding things forward.

TRIAL OUTLINE

as of _____, _____
Trial Date:
Theme:
Schedule Office Appointment with Witnesses
I   Discovery Cut-Off
II   Summary Judgment
III Witness List
IV Exhibit List
V   Motions
VI Motion in limine
VII Pre-trial Motions
VIII Voir Dire
IX Opening Statement
X   Plaintiff's Case
    A. Liability And Causation
       1.
    B. Damages
       1. Medical Doctors, etc.
          1a.
       2. Lay Witnesses who will corroborate Plaintiff's damages.
XI Motions Prior to Plaintiff's Rest, including motion that Pleadings Be Amended to Conform with Proof.
XII Anticipated Cross Examination
    A.

XIII Motions at Close of Defendants Case
XIV Closing Statement
    A.   Summation (must argue damages)
    B.   Rebuttal Argument
XV Jury Instructions
Format:

1. Tell the truth.

2. Practice. Practice, practice, practice.

22. TRIAL DATE

Why do cases settle?

Trial date.

The trial date is your friend.

Some might lament, "Why don't they just settle because it's the right thing to do?"

They just don't. Our adversarial system requires otherwise.

I've spent much of my life preparing for cases that don't get tried, that settle on the courthouse steps.

23. MEDICAL RECORD STIPULATIONS

Beware of stipulating that medical bills and records come in as a matter of course.

Prove the ones you need; make the other side do the same. Or, reach a written agreement exactly setting out what you are comfortable with.

It will bite you in the butt to agree to all meds coming in only to find out of a 20 year old horrible record you knew nothing about.

24. Depositions

Prepare for depositions as thoroughly as for trial.

Any deposition worth taking is worth taking by video; don't forget to notice it for video or risk an objection.

In this day and time of uncertainty, when defending a deposition of anyone other than your client, especially an expert, consider doing a "cross exam" that elicits facts and opinions necessary to establish a prima facie case. Conventional wisdom says a plaintiff lawyer shouldn't cross his own witness at a discovery deposition noticed by the defense, (to save it for trial). I agree if the witness is your client, but for almost every other witness who helps the cause, consider a cross examination which covers every issue necessary to establish a prima facie case. Your client will be at the trial. It's hard to guarantee that for anyone else. Things happen; people get sick; die; move; forget; get stranded flying across country; get lost; renege. Since you've told them through discovery every opinion the expert has, and since the defense has spent the money for the discovery deposition and now knows for sure all the opinions of the expert, go ahead and can them for playing to the jury at trial. You can still call the witness live if you want to (and I agree that in a perfect world live is better), but you have the insurance of the canned testimony if something goes wrong. Make sure to back up your trial presentation software and hardware, or risk a witness being stricken.

I think the trend is to take more depositions. At least that's been the trajectory of my practice.

Fail to depose an expert, and then watch at trial as the expert comes up with some outrageous theory not disclosed in the written discovery, and you'll tend to take more depositions. That's the primary reason for deposing all witnesses, especially experts.

The other reason is to create video clips that can be used in opening and closing arguments, and perhaps to help in cross examination. A video clip needs to be clean, so be sure when you hear a gem to inquire about it six ways from Sunday until your short simple question is answered with a short simple reply without objection.

I once asked a truck driver how he ingested methamphetamine. "I snorted it, I ate it, I put it in my Mountain Dew. I did everything but shoot it." That 15 second video clip was better than any two hour movie I could have made. Did I mention any deposition worth taking is worth taking by video?

We took 33 depositions in one case.

In a dram shop case, I am convinced the reason we were able to settle for significant policy limits was because after deposing every probable defense witness who could have known anything about what happened, and their all claiming no knowledge, we were left with the unchallenged testimony of the perpetrator who testified that he was served while visibly intoxicated, the linchpin question of the case.

25. Ask the Ultimate Question First

Monty Preiser taught me on deposition cross examination to ask the ultimate questions first. I tried it on some simple cases, and it seemed to be an okay plan. Then I tried it on a complex case and experienced the "aha" moment. When we start with reams of facts and a theory, we don't have the depth of understanding that would be necessary to cross examine an important witness, but by the time of cross exam we've gotten to know the minutiae. When you know the minutiae, there usually is one linchpin question. Ask it. From that point you know the facts and law so well that no matter what the witness says you will know what to do.

One reason doctors hate lawyers is because of 8 hour depositions. My doctor depositions usually do not last more than an hour or two.

26. CLIENT ATTENDANCE OF DEPOSITIONS

Should a client attend the depositions of other witnesses? Usually, clients don't attend depositions of others or the pre-trial hearings. However, when the client's doctor is being deposed I have found the outcome to be better if the client is present.

Any time you think a client's presence will better focus a witness or a court, have the client attend.

27. Interpreters, Bankers as Witnesses to Empower

A few years back we represented an Hispanic family. Their English was not much better than my Spanish. We warned them that by the time of trial they should be able to testify in English. That did not happen. Luckily I had learned on the Listserv from Ken Swindle not to worry. He sent me a go-by Motion in Limine to Exclude as Not Relevant Evidence of Nationality. Next I contacted the Supreme Court's Office of Interpreter Services and arranged for translators to attend the trial. The translators were awesome. Their professional presence added to the dignity of the Court and underscored the importance of the trial. To an outside observer it might have looked like the United Nations, with all the headphones, microphones, and suits. The clients were credible in their own right. That credibility was enhanced by the presence of the translators.

Similarly, consider having a guardian of the estate (banker) testify when you represent a minor or ward. Your asking the guardian about the legitimate use of court ordered funds paid into a court monitored account will go a long way with a jury.

Do not forget that juries impute your professionalism, or lack thereof, to your clients.

Local counsel can be invaluable in jury selection and in fostering relations with the court.

I view hiring local counsel the same way I look at hiring a CPA to help with taxes—ideally they'll save you more than you pay them.

There are a million things to know about voir dire. Here are my top 3.

1. Let them know how you feel about jury service (second only to military service in time of war for civic duties). To do this I tell the Milas Hale story—the story of how when I was 26 years old a potential client came to our offices trying to hire an attorney to get him out of jury service. I left the client in my office while I went to consult with Milas. "You tell that man to get out of here, that he should be ashamed to try to shirk his civic duty, that we won't have anything to do with it." As Milas' red face began to return to normal he said, "Also tell him being a juror is a wonderful experience, and he will be glad he did it." I remind the jury that Jefferson said, "The jury vote is more important than the right to vote at the polls—because a jury vote is a direct vote; rather than a vote for a representative." Then let them know that you will help them to be excused, if necessary.

2. Insurance. Do you or anyone in your immediate family work for an insurance company? Ad infinitum.

3. When you sit down, there should be nothing left for opposing counsel to discuss that you have not discussed already, leaving little with which to gain rapport that wouldn't be repetitive.

Also, try this: Go down the list numerically. Call each juror by name, and ask a couple of questions about them or their family. As new jurors are called to replace those excused by the Court, ask a couple of questions of each new juror by name. It is obvious, but the process establishes a personal relationship that a general voir dire addressed to the entire panel misses. Don't forget that referring to jurors by name after voir dire is improper argument.

Talk to other attorneys regarding opposing counsel's usual voir dire from their previous cases. Like us, defense attorneys use over and over again what works for them. When we can preemptively use their arguments, it throws defense counsel off kilter and thus improves our client's position.

Voir dire is when you plant your Golden Rule seeds. "Ever made a mistake? What did you do about it? Did you admit it? Fix it?"

Get juror promises regarding no sympathy, so that you can remind in summation that sympathy cuts both ways—not to have sympathy for the defendant when assessing damages. "It's your job to assess the verdict; it's my job to collect it."

Many years ago I was leaving the courthouse in Greene County, tail between my legs, having just lost a rear-end collision case for a little old lady, a case that shouldn't have been lost. I hadn't spared any expense. I thought I had asked all the right questions, but I knew, and the bailiff knew, that the only thing that had kept my client from a plaintiff's verdict was the inexperience of her lawyer and sympathy for the defendant.

The bailiff walked me to my car relating the story of Lawyer Brown.

"He would always ask in voir dire if the jurors would not let sympathy play a part in the verdict. Then in closing argument he'd remind them of their promise, with the further admonition: Don't you worry about the defendant or how the verdict will be paid. That's not your job. Your job is to assess the verdict. It's my job to collect it."

I realized I had to do a better job of discussing sympathy in closing statement—and in order to do that I had to do a better job of laying the foundation in voir dire. The process of laying the foundation in voir dire, getting commitments, and then following through with the if/then analysis in summation is important for every important issue of the case.

When I got back in the office the next day I called one of the jurors I had felt a strong connection with to ask how I could improve things for the next trial. "Oh, you did fine, and we liked your client. We just felt sorry for Bobby" (the defendant, real party in interest).

"Didn't you realize insurance was involved? Do you remember my voir dire questions regarding whether anyone worked for an insurance company?"

"No, we didn't know that."

I now talk about insurance in voir dire until the judge tells me to move on.

"What is your favorite activity?" (Plaintiff can't do that.)

"Who is someone who was a positive influence on you when you were growing up?" Who taught you the Golden Rule? Was he or she a reasonable person? (In close you can ask what a reasonable person would have done). Remember, Golden Rule references in voir dire are not argument. They might later remember this question as they're deliberating—and you haven't argued the Golden Rule.

Refer to your heroes—grandparents, etc. Let the values you seek to enforce emanate from those who obviously influenced you and at the same time bringing to juror's minds thoughts and memories of their parents'—and grandparents'—values. Ask about their values with regard to the critical elements of the trial.

Would you file a lawsuit to protect your rights if someone negligently caused you harm?" (You can't ask the question in closing arguments, but in voir dire it's not Golden Rule argument).

Make a mini opening, but don't call it that; just ease into it. Introduce arguments and rhetorical devices.

Be careful introducing the theme too soon so not to invite a counter theme to debunk.

Introduce in voir dire the characters you'll be quoting in close.

Get them to talk—use the time to connect jurors to the case via their personal experiences. If a conversation isn't flowing, ask more open ended questions. It's okay to remind them voir dire is the only time in the trial they get to speak out loud.

How do you *feel* about?

Use sentence completion, e.g., "red, yellow, black, and _____."

If applicable, teach. Explain the effects of a 50/50 verdict. Explain the effect of the medical negligence statute, the *requirement* of expert witnesses, their cost, etc.

Treat opposing counsel like he or she doesn't exist.

Embrace "frivolous lawsuits." Nobody likes frivolous lawsuits. Distinguish your case. I ask for a show of hands of anyone who has heard that there are too many frivolous lawsuits. Keep your composure as they almost all raise a hand. (Indeed note the ones who don't. Someone who won't participate with a simple request might be harder to persuade). Next ask for a show of hands of anyone who really believes there are too many frivolous lawsuits. Talk to and later burn your peremptory challenges on the most vocal. Then distinguish your client's plight from frivolous lawsuits. "Would it be a frivolous lawsuit if someone died in a hospital of an easily treatable condition but the doctors and hospital failed to recognize and treat? Would a death under those circumstances be frivolous to you?"

Do talk about prejudice.

Smile.

Ask jurors for help. E.g., "Would you like for me to arrange for my client to be in the courtroom one day so that you can meet her, even though she can't speak, can't be here every day?"

Explain that Jury instructions are the *law of the case—and seek commitments* that the jurors agree to *follow the law*.

1. **Attention! Grab her!** Say something to get and hold their attention. Maybe mention the theme. Present tense is good—mention of the date of incident, time, weather, (seasons), sights, sounds, and smells, things that help the jury to see and feel the big picture.

2. **Roadmap of the Case.** Highlight the favorable points (short of arguing). Preemptively bring out the negatives.

3. Tell them what you want them to do (without getting an objection for argument).
   - Do not use notes. Have your case divided into a 3 part outline and speak from the heart.
   - Do use video clips if the Court will allow. (Some courts allow it as a matter of course; some never; usually it's best to get pre-authorization with a motion).
   - Attain credibility as a teacher who will tell the truth.
   - Practice, preferably to a mock judge and jury; in front of a mirror, at least.
   - Show photos of the experts as you introduce witnesses.
   - Opening statement is when most trial lawyers say a case is won or lost. (I think it happens in voir dire).

31. Listening to the Answers to Examination Questions and Following Through

We have all seen it. The lawyer who reads the questions carefully prepared for the witness examination and then, when offered up the response that begs the follow through slam dunk question, the lawyer misses the moment and reads instead the next question written out on the legal pad.

Try preparing your examination in outline form rather than preparing in advance each question to be asked. Cover a topic, listening to the responses and following through. Repeating in question form the information just given you invites the witness to expound, but the main point to remember is to *listen* and then to follow through.

For example, a question that should be asked of a defendant driver in every vehicle collision case is, "Were you using a cell phone at the time of the wreck?"

If the answer is, "Yes," follow through with who, what, when, where, and why. For how long? Pleasant/angry? Excited/not excited? Witness? Distracted? What did each of you say at the time of the wreck? Who is your cell phone service provider?

If "No," follow through with "Did you have a cell phone in the vehicle with you?" "Was it turned on?" "Were you text messaging or using email?" "When was the last time you had used the cell phone?" "Were you holding the cell phone at the time of the wreck?" "Where was the cell phone?" "Cradled or loose?" "Did you use the cell phone after the wreck to call anyone?" "Whom?"

"What phone number?" "How long after the wreck?" "What is the assigned number of your cell phone with area code?" "Will you please sign this release to allow me to get your cell phone records?"

You can think of even more questions, depending upon the answers to each additional question.

Just do not be the one who asks, "Were you using a cell phone?" and then follow through with, "What was the weather like that day?"

1. **Practice.** Make your client and witnesses look and sound good.

2. **Practice.** Mine facts for the theme and closing arguments.

3. **Practice.** Empower your client and witnesses to admit freely, if asked, the fact they did discuss their testimony with you and that you advised them to tell the truth.

1. Get them to agree on the incontrovertible facts that favor your case.

2. Poke holes where you can.

3. Show their bias; ask about their personal interest/payment for testifying.

Show a bit of your soul. Mention someone you have loved.

You can and should argue the effects of comparative fault, but beware of arguing to the jury *how* to arrive at their verdict. The model instructions handle that for you. Arguing for a quotient verdict can be reversible error.

Remember that in order to argue damages in rebuttal, you must have argued damages in summation.

Some defense lawyers will object to your arguing damages in rebuttal if the defense chose not to argue damages in their summation; however, I've never had a judge not allow Plaintiff's damages to be argued in rebuttal as long as damages were argued in Plaintiff's summation.

Remind the jury that the instructions are the law of the case, that they promised in voir dire to follow the law.

Walk the walk. If you talk about better to be an hour early than a minute late, be sure that you are early to court.

Use all your rhetorical devices, but especially the embedded command. "If you find in favor of (Plaintiff), you must award damages."

I like to mention the duties of everyone in the court room. The duty of the Judge to see to a fair trial; the duty of the lawyers to represent their clients zealously; the duty of the jurors to be attentive and impartial; the duty of the Defendant, which was breached.

35. JURY INSTRUCTIONS

Do not wait till the deadline to prepare jury instructions. Prepare them as soon as you file the lawsuit, so that you can visualize what you have to prove.

As a Plaintiff's attorney, when possible, I usually prefer a general verdict form rather than to submit the verdict on interrogatories.

My graduation from law school coincided with the passing of Frank Cox's father. Frank asked me to handle the few remaining litigation cases. During one of those trials I learned a lesson that has served me well since.

The trial seemed to be going our way. I was a little taken aback when, at the end of the first day of trial, the judge requested a trial brief. But I burned the midnight oil and did it.

In this day and time of motions to dismiss, motions for summary judgment, and motions ad nauseam, almost every issue is briefed. But if you find yourself in a situation where that's not the case, I highly recommend a trial brief that covers all anticipated issues. In addition to providing focus and authority, it unnerves the other side if they failed to prepare one.

We won that case. Not long after, the person we had sued hired me to handle his legal affairs. I suppose that was one of the highest compliments about practicing law that I ever received.

"Tuesday at 10 till trial" is easy to remember. It employs the power of three and alliteration. It helps with focus. It's toward the first of the week but not on a Monday.

When in trial mode (at least the 30 days preceding a trial) everyone in our office knows that, court schedule permitting, everyone assigned to the case will be meeting at least every Tuesday at 10 AM till the trial.

The clients are made aware of these meetings and invited to attend.

When an individual has to miss for any reason, the others meet regardless.

Some variation of "Tuesday at 10 till trial" is highly recommended.

Associate an appellate specialist early on, to help during trial and be ready for appeal.

Anticipate appellate land mines. E.g., in a medical negligence case make sure your liability witnesses are well versed regarding the locality rule.

Moot oral arguments.

Depending upon your confidence level regarding trial errors, now might be a good time for another mediation.

39. Talk about Money

People put off till last talking about money. (We were taught it's usually not polite to speak about money).

It's hard to talk about money unless your cause is just.

It's the first thing I talk about in a job interview—if the money's not right the other stuff seldom matters.

I normally talk about money from the get-go and let the jury know it's ok if the cause is just. Sometimes I'm vague about it on purpose in voir dire so that the defense can't attack a specific number. Qualifying in voir dire that a jury can agree to consider "millions and millions of dollars" lets you get the commitment to consider high numbers but leaves nothing specific to attack.

40. Look a Jury in the Eyes

I had positioned myself 50 paces away from the opening gate, where the bulls begin their half mile charge to the arena. I planned to stay in front of them. I arrived an hour early, before the barricades were sealed. Neither I nor most of the crowd knew the drill. Looking back, there had been a one minute warning rocket, followed by the release of the lead steers and then the bulls. But that didn't matter. Once the warning rocket fired, the sea of people within the barricades started to roll like a Saturday night crowd on Bourbon Street during Mardi Gras. There was no control, no ability to maneuver or run. The best I could do was keep my footing on the cobblestones, slick from spilled wine and urine.

Pandemonium let loose with the bulls. The bulls clambered on the cobblestones. Drunks ran in the wrong direction, toward the bulls. The rest of us were squeezed forward on the relatively wide street, eventually into the narrow chute tunnel into the arena.

Blood dripped down an arm. People wearing white with red sashes escorted a stumbling runner wearing white, splattered with blood, out from the tunnel. I tried to flatten myself against the sides of the tunnel walls as the thundering herd of hooves swooshed through the middle, exiting the tunnel into the arena, sucking the remainder in its wake. Any blood on me came from others.

There was mass confusion as runners and bulls sought out their places in the arena. The runners were looking to escape by climbing over the arena walls. The bulls, dangerously confused, were being half herded and half led to another gate, opposite where we'd all entered the arena. The general plan was for the bulls to run across the arena and then through the far gate to await the bull fights; the runners into the stands and back into life.

There was an unprotected bench-like perimeter that gave a leg up to runners trying to exit the arena. As I stood on it, I was slightly below and almost face to face with spectators on the other side of the wall who were shoulder to shoulder, protecting their front row positions, not willing to move.

I could tell by looking in their eyes most enjoyed the dominance; perhaps one was along for the ride; and finally my gaze met one who felt sorry for me and took a half step back. That was all I needed. Palms on the top of the wall, arms stiff, I plunged my torso into the opening, while over my shoulder I could see the bulls finally were running pell-mell into their intended gate. As I tumbled into the stands my steel-toed shoes kicked a couple of the spectators who would have enjoyed seeing me gored.

You've got to look a jury in the eyes the same way. You look at one and don't let go until the next one is in your gaze. You don't let that one go till the next one engages.

During voir dire let them know it's ok to wink or raise a hand to let you know if they need help, and that you will help get their concern to the judge.

I didn't stick around to play with the baby bulls let loose in the arena. My quest was done. I set out to find my family who, because of the masses, had not been able to make it to the viewing balcony we had rented. Hours later, after getting lost In *Pamplona*'s maze, I met them back at the hotel. We were all relieved, none more than I.

We were ready to go. We had loved the experience, the paella served from a cauldron, the manchego, the late night dinner with sangria, the bright yellow eggs for breakfast, the spectacle of red sashes and white clothing, the challenge of the run, the stories of those who had run before and came back just for the party. But the slick cobblestones, the drunks, and the congestion of humanity went a long way in a short while.

And It never hurts for opposing counsel to think you might be a little crazy.

Congratulate the other side on the verdict.
Advise your client what's next.
Be the first person at the office the next day.
When you win, same drill.

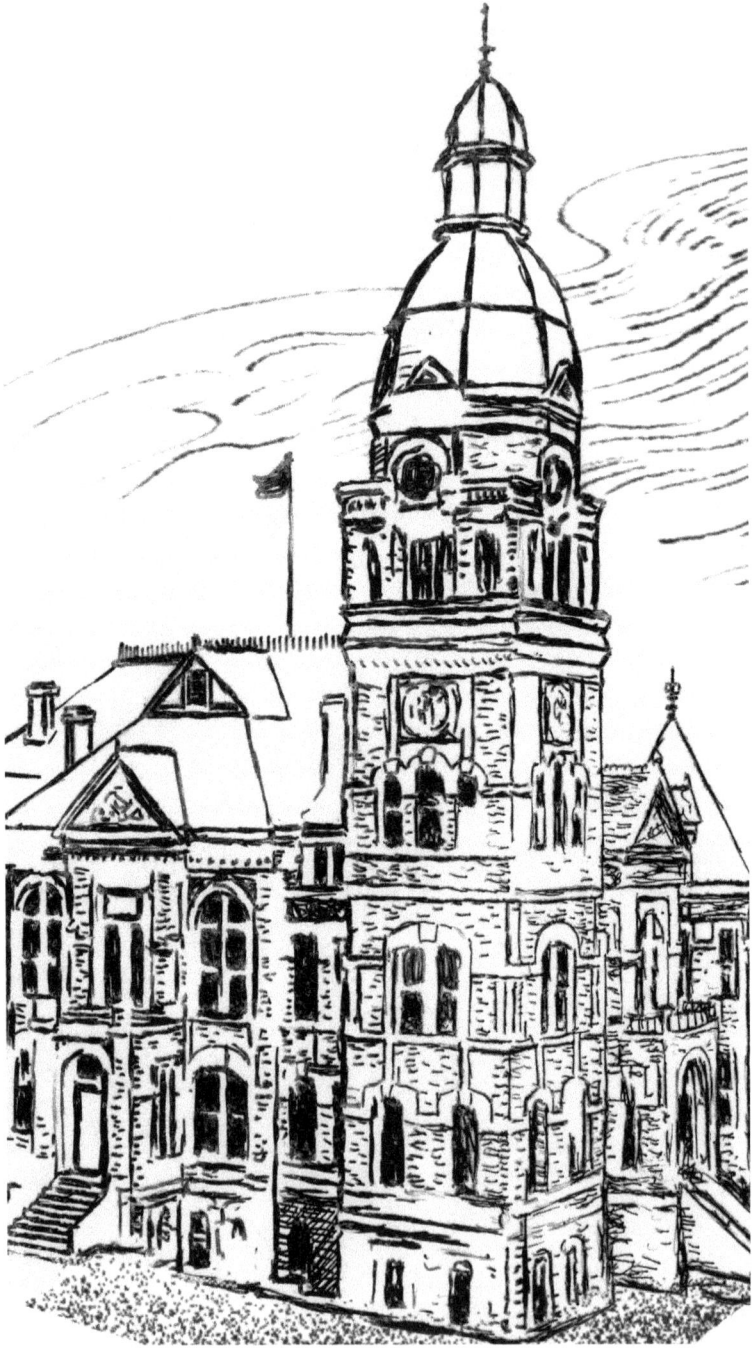

III. Everything Else

42. KEEP IT SIMPLE

Once a friend was sued for fraud in a complex securities action. I knew my friend could and would sell ice to Eskimos just to prove he could do it, but that he wouldn't defraud anyone.

I didn't understand the securities transaction. The math was way over my head. I fretted about it to co-counsel Stuart Hankins.

"Gary, the jury will understand. It's no different than buying a gallon of milk at the grocery store. If they didn't like your price, they could have gone somewhere else."

That became my closing statement.

"If they didn't like the price of milk at the Corner Grocery they could've gone to Kroger."

My client enjoyed a defense verdict on the multi-million dollar claim against him, and the jury assessed a verdict in his favor for his counterclaim for outrage; but we lost that one on appeal.

To set up this story I've got to tell you about Patricia the way I'd tell a jury panel in voir dire about how important jury service is and then let them know notwithstanding that, I would help them get their concerns to the judge in an attempt to get them excused from service.

Patricia is my world. Where she goes I will go. Her people are my people. That she sees something in me is the highest compliment of my life. When she invited me to join her to walk over 500 miles on a pilgrimage route to Santiago de Compostela, I said, "Of course," though I didn't know where Santiago de Compostela was. It was an easy choice, 37 days with her or 37 days without her.

Patricia is by far my better half. She is smart, beautiful, kind, loving, and fun. I'm the luckiest guy in the world because I get to go to bed every night with the woman of my dreams.

Awards are like hemorrhoids—sooner or later every asshole gets one. It was my turn. I got up to say a few words. I thanked the organization, made a quip or two, one about being considerate and keeping it brief, then sat down, thinking I'd done ok. Patricia had given me a smile as I walked back to our table. That was all that mattered.

Then someone else got an award, and about the only thing talked about was how the significant other was the one who should have been up there, being so supportive and wonderful and all. I asked Patricia how she felt about that speech, the one that glorified and acknowledged the significant other. She said it had been, "a nice touch." I felt like a heel and don't think I could have slunk any lower in my chair.

I've not held back, telling you about trials I lost, in hopes that you won't make the same mistakes. Put this mistake of mine at the top of the list of things not to do. If you're lucky enough to have a muse, a partner, the best in the world mock juror, exalt and acknowledge her or him.

It's better not to make them, but when you do, fix your mistakes, the sooner the better.

44. NEXT

What's next?

What's next to advance your career, to plan your life?

What's your plan for ten years out?

Long-range goal setting was not of interest or importance to me until someone stated the obvious and told me why it's a good idea. Just as a good warning requires the person being warned to understand why, an admonition for long-range planning tends to fall on deaf ears, even to be resented, unless we understand why a long-term goal is advisable. It's advisable because of the focus it gives us. To look ten years out on a plane or graph focuses us on that goal; everything else is peripheral. A long-term goal is a rifle shot aimed at what we want to happen.

45. LAW FIRM MANAGEMENT

Law firm management might sound sexy to the uninitiated. After all, it's an honor to lead, to manage. But the reality is that management is hard, time-consuming work.

At one time I was a partner in an eight partner law firm. Each of the eight of us, at one time or another, proudly undertook the responsibility of being managing partner. But soon, after taking all we could take of the mundane part of a law practice, we would earnestly try to convince the next attorney that he was the best one to fill the management job shoes. It lasted a few years, with many managing partners; then attrition took its toll.

Some people are sales people. Some are management material. Seldom is one as good at one job as the other. The same goes for practicing law and managing a law firm. The smaller the firm, the higher the chance of having no choice but to practice law and to manage the practice of law. But at some point, management becomes full time. At some point, the focus necessary to try a jury trial or to complete a complex transaction precludes the ability to successfully manage. Managing lawyers is akin to herding cats. Managers do well to keep filled the real estate allotted to them and are lucky if they can attract good people to make themselves seem good managers.

In my final analysis, a good manager must be a hardworking and good organizer who can inspire by example and adapt daily to the ever changing landscape. Good managers reasonably allow themselves to become educated and enthused, implement, make mistakes and then recognize and fix those mistakes, and then move on to the next challenge.

Something I learned from Herschel Friday: make rounds every morning. Say hello, to everyone. When it's time to leave for the day, say good-bye to anyone still there.

Something I learned the hard way: it's best to have a no rehire policy. Someone who will quit you once will quit you again. You can couple that with a "no comment" policy to avoid future defamation lawsuits and that, "Would you hire them again?" question from those seeking references.

46. POLICIES AND PROCEDURES

A good friend taught me procedures must be put in place to implement policy. There should be no policy without a procedure in place to implement the policy. That sounds simple enough, but before receiving that advice our policy and procedure manuals were not very well related.

Keep that in mind and get started.

Keep up with the stuff that bears repeating and place it in the manuals.

Review manuals developed by others and keep the good stuff.

Realize the manuals will grow and be continuously changing. Respect them. Enforce them. Improve them.

Realize your policies and procedures might be used against you someday in litigation. Indeed, some avoid formal policies and procedures for this reason. But I urge you to develop a good set, which you'll find helpful in training and in preserving and communicating your institutional knowledge.

When I consider all the sub-files and sub-categories utilized in computer design, I realize I am not very organized as compared to the geniuses who design computer programs. However, before the electronic world, there was an old school of organization which deserves repeating:

The three most important tools to assist in organization are a desk, an alphabetical filing cabinet, and a trash basket. When something comes across the desk, one of three things should be done with it: Work on it right then, file it, or throw it away. Right then means the same day it comes across the desk; otherwise, it should be filed to be worked on at a later time (or thrown away).

I keep a miscellaneous file and a miscellaneous inchoate file. The miscellaneous inchoate file is used for filing things that I intend to return to within the next few days or weeks (and which do not yet deserve a file of their own).

Those in our offices with cluttered desks are cautioned that if they cannot find something, they cannot work on it. They are further cautioned that we do not have time continuously to be searching for lost things or files.

Lawyers are taught that despite what they might think or attempt to rationalize, a cluttered desk suggests a cluttered mind, not the mind a client wants to pay big bucks to.

Soon after a solo practice becomes a small office, a central filing system should be considered. It might not be the ticket for every office, but with multiple people potentially needing access to the same files, those files should be easily and centrally accessible.

Just as the introduction of a time clock meets resistance and is necessary when an office starts to grow, the introduction and preservation of a central filing system will meet resistance. Perseverance will be necessary to prevent resistant individuals from creating their own personal filing system within their own offices.

Act immediately, file, or throw away.

48. Never Ending Tort Reform

They do it because: 1) "It might save me a nickel," and 2) "It protects me to the extent I'm a defendant (get sued)."

We resist because: 1) "It is anti-consumer, disguised as anti-lawyer," and 2) "It negatively affects my constitutional rights."

I have found the best way to communicate the seriousness of ever morphing tort reform is with this quote:

> *"Judicial reform is no sport for the short-winded."*
> — Arthur T. Vanderbilt, May 5, 1957

49. MAKING A DECISION

Most good management decisions tend to make themselves. If you study a problem enough and pay attention, a good decision evolves.

The most important part of making a decision is to just do it. Don't dwell on the decision. Whatever you decide, then implement. It will be okay. If later you determine with new data the course needs to be changed, that's okay too. We all make mistakes—successful people fix (or sell) their mistakes.

When you're trying to make something happen and you're dealing with other people who have to make a decision, get to the point of "Are you in or out?"

If you're waiting on someone, "In or out?"

"The time for deadlines has passed. Are you in or out?"

"In or out?" allows you to get on down the road, to stop wasting time. "In or out" forces a decision from one reluctant to commit.

Make decisions. Move on. Fix mistakes.

50. Privileged Communications & Client Confidences

Whether we represent someone is privileged. Avoid having clients sit in a common waiting room. Escort them from the reception area to a conference room or office as soon as possible.

Knowing that at times there are clients or others in our offices, make sure that confidential documents that are on desk or counter tops are turned face down.

We learn in law school the importance of client confidentiality. It is our duty to share that information with staff.

51. Learn How to Say No

We cannot be all things to all people. If we say yes to everything we become inundated. If we put off saying no when that's the appropriate thing to do, we create unnecessary confusion, expectations, and stress.

To be clear, to make sure your message is heard, say no unequivocally on the front end; give your reasons later.

Be resolute. Unless additional compelling information is offered, don't reconsider. Those who want to suck you into their sink hole can be very persuasive, very persistent.

A cause of action is either an asset or a liability. When we begin working up a case, we think it has the potential to be an asset, but the moment we realize it is not, for whatever reason, it has become a liability. Once a cause of action is determined to be a liability, it should be exited as soon as possible, properly closed, with a written notice to the clients, documenting the facts of closing and warning of any necessary action the clients should be made aware. Only then does the statute of limitations begin to run on whatever perceived mistakes we might have made.

Every day we have to make decisions regarding which battles we are going to fight. There are more battles then we have time left on earth to fight. So, we must choose our battles, and we must choose them wisely.

Saying no to a would-be litigant for a case we do not believe in is essential if we are to be successful and if we are to have time to devote to the causes we do believe in.

Learn to say no early on, leaving no room for confusion about having said no.

We have a policy at our office that once we decline a case for whatever reason (and have properly notified the client in writing, etc.), we will not again consider the matter. Sometimes we let good cases get away, but the ability to have finality, recognized and respected by everyone who works in our office, is worth more than what we might miss.

Also, once a decision to close a file has been made and the closing protocol implemented, that liability has been dealt with. For another lawyer in the firm to second guess the first lawyer who closed the file or for a lawyer to be changing his or her mind takes what has been determined to be a liability and reopens the proverbial can of worms. If you let that happen the statute of limitations for professional negligence starts to run again, the closing protocol has to be complied with once again, and a demanding client has prevailed upon you when your first instinct was to say no.

52. LETTER TO A STUDENT

1234 ABC Lane
Little Rock, AR 72201

October 14, 2002

Mr. Gary Green
Law Offices of Gary Green
2311 Biscayne Drive
Little Rock, AR 72207

Dear Mr. Green:

As a student with future plans to pursue law, I find it imperative that I research and uncover much knowledge about the profession before delving into it. I would greatly appreciate your help in learning about present and future opportunities for determined students.

Enclosed you will find a questionnaire and return envelope. I would be very thankful if you would take a moment out of your hectic schedule to reply to my enquiries; this is important in my decisions toward future schooling and a profession in law.

Respectfully,

John C. Doe

Enclosures

Gary Green
Law Offices of Gary Green
November 6, 2002

Career Questionnaire

1. *What were your ambitions as a youth, and at what point in your life did you realize that you wanted to be a lawyer?*
    A. When my father strongly suggested it.

2. *Was it difficult to begin your own law firm?*
    A. No.

3. *Who was an inspiration or role model of yours and why?*
    A. My father, because he was not educated formally but wanted me to be. My mother and grandparents for the unconditional love they gave and taught me. My wife still inspires me. My children still inspire and motivate me. Fellow trial lawyers. Leaders.

4. *Do you sense a great deal of competition between other law firms and yours? Or rather companionship?*
    A. Both. More competition.

5. *What high school and college courses do you feel best prepared you for your career?*
    A. I don't think the schools matter that much. Its more hard work and desire. You already communicate well, and that's what is most important.

Good luck to you. There's always room for a good lawyer!

Gary Green

Cases tend to settle toward the end of the calendar year because most insurance companies pay taxes based on the calendar year. Add to that the fact that insurance companies are required to establish an estimated "reserve" loss for any claim of which they have knowledge, then one can understand the end of the year rush experienced by personal injury law firms. A claim reserved at $20,000 that settles for $12,000 just increased the company's bottom line by $8,000, as far as the accountants, regulators and investors are concerned.

We can help our clients by realizing this and positioning their cases to be in the negotiation phase (and calling those adjusters) before, rather than after year end. Rest assured that cases which do not get settled by year end and that do not have the benefit of an early in the year trial date, will not be seriously considered again by the insurance company until next year's end or until the presence of an imminent trial date.

Why do we not use the word "accident" in our offices? Because the word conjures up the idea that no one was at fault. If we use the word among ourselves, that habit could slip into the courtroom, where words are critical.

The same logic applies to other words. In the past, I have been guilty of following the insurance industry's lead in using "soft tissue injury" to describe an injury short of a fracture. "Soft tissue injury" conjures up the impression of a bruise. The word does not fit well the ligamentous and connective tissue injuries suffered by many of our clients.

Try referring to chiropractors and family practice or general practice doctors as primary care doctors. That description better connotes early treatment of trauma and the subsequent referral to others, if warranted.

When the defense requires our client, pursuant to statute, to undergo a medical exam, we should not follow their lead by referring to the exam as an "IME" or "independent medical exam." It is a compulsory medical exam, or perhaps even better, a defense medical exam. This is such a strong notion that one should consider a motion in limine to prevent the defense from referring to compulsory exams as an IME or independent medical exam.

Medical "malpractice" sounds worse (and harder to prove) then medical "negligence."

"The doctor ran a medical red light" sounds like medical negligence. "The doctor intentionally or badly caused harm" sounds more like medical "malpractice."

Be mindful of the power of words, in and out of the courtroom.

55. Being There

My office manager asked me how I managed the small stuff. How did I address those who clock in and then proceed to have breakfast in the kitchen on company time, those who are addicted to social media, those who abuse break time, etc.?

Of course, we have in place policy manuals and checks and balances for keeping up with attendance. But my best answer to that question was, "By being there."

The first and most important thing that we do if we manage well is to hire good people. The second most important thing we do is to be there, to lead by example, to motivate, to break up with our presence the Monday morning replays. One of my first mentors taught me the importance of being the first to arrive in the morning and the last to leave in the evening.

Being there when it is quiet is just as important as being there during the hub bub of activity, and being there during the hub bub of activity is critical.

Being there empathetically is easy when someone is having a difficult time in their life—tell them to come back when they can, and until then you will cover for them. It is understood that this cover will only be provided within reason, and I have never seen it abused.

Being there for a loan of money can prove your friendship and your loyalty to an employee, but there should be an understanding of how the loan is to be repaid, and, in general, a loan should be expected to be repaid from booked earnings. Being there means making payroll when you don't get paid yourself.

Being there means you plan to be there come hell or high water and that if someone helps you along the way, they will not be forgotten.

Being there means that in inclement weather, after a personal crisis, after losing a trial, or in times of a national emergency you plan to be at work. You plan to keep on keeping on no matter what.

Being there means letting key personnel know their job is secure, no matter what mistakes we all are bound to make even when we are trying our best.

Stress affects everyone differently. Some thrive on it while others cannot tolerate it. Too much stress causes problems. Obviously a law firm can be an extremely stressful place. It is up to us to know how much stress we can tolerate and to structure our lives accordingly. Following are some suggestions that might help:

1. Don't say you can do something when you can't.
2. Learn how and when to say no to demands for your time.
3. Prepare for the next deadline well before the deadline.
4. Get organized.
5. Have the mindset that you are going to exercise every day. There'll be days when you can't, but at least do daily calisthenics.
6. This suggestion is a double edged sword, but consider working some extra time to get caught up.
7. Spend time away from work to "re-charge."
8. Take a hot bath.
9. Take deep breaths.
10. Limit caffeine.
11. Close files now that have no merit or value.
12. Limit "dead time" by anticipating it. Take work with you to a doctor's appointment, etc.
13. Use standard forms. Don't reinvent the wheel.
14. Plant a garden, or develop another hobby.
15. Take yourself off the call list for a while if you feel overwhelmed.

16. Eat a balanced diet.
17. Have a drink or two. Enjoy things in moderation. Hangovers and bad health cause more stress.
18. Don't cross examine the spouse, or otherwise bring the stress of the office home with you. Sometimes it's a good idea to decompress before going home.
19. Ask a friend to lunch.
20. Enjoy a massage.
21. Be positive. Things aren't bad unless we think them so. Enjoy where you work and be proud of where you work or find some other place to work.

57. SUCCESS

Success is loving what you do, doing it well and not thinking about the money. The money will come if you love what you do and do it well. Nothing novel here, but if you don't realize success has nothing to do with the accumulation of money, you'll be disappointed.

Success can be thought of as a huge map. The final destination or goal is success. What is important is to know that it is where you want to go and your next step. Realize you are going to get there if you set out to get there, figure out a general route and then get started. It does not matter that things change along the way as long as you know you are going to get there. Indeed, do not get caught up in the details of the general route; just get started.

Commit to do whatever it takes.

If you do it because, by gosh, you said you're going to do it, you'll be successful. Of course you've got to be moral, you've got to think smart, and seize your luck, but it's very simple to be successful.

Don't forget the work. But it's simple.

To be successful, do what you do for the right reasons—because you are passionate about it, because you want to help others.

Know the big picture; tend to the necessary details.

Never think you might not be successful. Plan for the long run. Decide what it is you plan to do, say you are going to do it. Take the first step. Follow through.

107

Invest in your marketing.

All lawyers that are in practice market and advertise themselves in some way. Even before lawyers were allowed to advertise they'd remind other lawyers at the courthouse, somewhat tongue in cheek, to, "Sue my clients."

The key is to develop a calloused ego and to develop expertise within a niche.

Advertising works, so you'd better be good at what you do. Even bad advertising works.

Future business comes from the good job you do on what you've got. One of my biggest verdicts spawned from a divorce handled successfully the year before. A penny doubled every day hits a million dollars within one month. Good work ripples similarly.

One trick is to relate advertising to a percentage of your gross income. Realize the percentage should start high in your early years, and, if the advertising is good, well placed, etc., taper down to an industry accepted percentage of gross.

The question, "If I have to choose among all the available mediums and only want to choose one, which should I choose?" is a naive question. Advertising mediums integrate and work together to complement each other. Will yellow page advertising alone produce results? Yes. Will yellow page advertising complemented with television produce even better results than the same money spent only on television or yellow pages? Yes. Will throwing in a web page help even more? Of course. Search engine optimization and buying ad words? Yes. How about some signage? Yep. Radio? Works, too. Etc., Etc., Etc.

Canned commercials or your own mug? Both work. I prefer the straightforwardness of my own mug, but consider your privacy.

Continuous or continual? Remember paragraph one. Advertising works. Go continuously and negotiate for annual contracts.

Go with an advertising agency, place my own directly, or create my own agency? Start with an agency and eventually create your own agency to take advantage of the 15% traditionally paid to agencies by the advertising providers. Before you open your own agency, beware an agency that charges you more than 15%.

Take advantage of the television station's offer to produce commercials for no charge or hire a director and film your own commercials? Create and film your own.

Rely upon the art department of the yellow page and newspaper providers or provide your own art work at your expense? The key here is to develop a comprehensive specifications list of all print ads that possibly will be used and then use those exclusively until the spec pages change. An agency or yellow page broker can help with this, but make sure only one company is keeping the spec pages for your continual approval and editing.

Logo? Yes.

Mission statement? Yes.

Slogans? Yes.

Realize there will be changes over time. For me, "Don't Go to a Lawyer" became "We Make House Calls" became "A People's Practice." I'm sometimes reminded of a jingle that we haven't used in years but that people sometimes still sing to us in greeting. Yes, jingles work, too.

(There can be confusion in the clutter. I've been called Gary Miller at the grocery store. Gary Eubanks and I have laughed about clients calling on one of us thinking they were calling the other.)

Realize those who have responded favorably to your marketing and advertising once are more inclined than others to do so again (and can be reached much more inexpensively the second time than the first).

Your advertising and marketing needs to be something you can be proud of. Needs to be something that helps your particular clients.

Your advertising needs to be something more than, "Call me."

Any particular advertising needs to work synergistically with your other advertising. Never forget that marketing and advertising are just the first part of the equation. You have to follow through with quality work, or all that marketing and advertising are for naught.

So, to try to better answer the question of what is the most important advertising I have done:

1. Jury verdicts;
2. Word of mouth; and
3. The synergistic effect of combined marketing.

The mailing list—that list of people who already have called on you. They are the people most likely to call you in the future. You have spent lots of dollars to persuade them to be on the mailing list in the first place. Already, they have chosen you over the other hundreds of attorneys available to them. They already have demonstrated they respond to your marketing. When one considers the hundreds of dollars expended to generate one call, the importance of that caller becomes more apparent. The receptionist has to be nice to them. People taking the calls must be pleasant and display a caring attitude. And, even if you cannot help them now, they will call on you in the future, when you can help them, if you gently remind them with holiday cards, birthday cards, and occasional letters regarding issues of importance to them and their circle of friends.

Maybe this is the most important aspect of marketing for a professional to understand.

Greg Ferguson likes to tell this story. On one of his first days as a licensed lawyer he came to watch one of my morning stints in district court as a deputy public defender. Because he was wearing a tie, a man walked up to him. "You must be a lawyer. How much will you charge me to represent me this morning, so that I don't have to use the public defender?" Greg told the man he'd be right back and then came over to where I was. "How much do I charge him?"

"How much does he have?"

"I'll be right back."

"He says he has $50."

"I'd charge him $50. With that and a couple of small cases, you'll have a good week."

After my public defender days I did a lot of flat fee and hourly work. On the few cases that I handled through jury trial on an hourly basis, the fee was pretty steep. I was already trying to move to flat fee or percentage fees even in the general practice work I was doing, having noticed my accounts receivable going up and aging.

Then I picked up a lagniappe. One of my partners, John Ward, was appointed by Governor Clinton to serve out the circuit court judgeship term of Judith Rogers, who had won election to the Arkansas Court of Appeals. John asked if I would handle to completion the forty or so personal injury cases he did not have time to finish. It was one of the best things that ever happened to me. It involved trial work. The clients surely needed help. The money would be good if I worked hard and smart and was lucky. And there were no accounts receivable. By the time I finished those cases I was hooked.

I respect those who bill hourly and realize hourly billing avoids the zero pay days, and the windfalls. But the contingent fee is the poor man's key to the courthouse, and I wouldn't have much to work on if I didn't offer contingency fee contracts. Indeed, I'm even noticing business people inquiring about contingency fees recently, saying they want someone with skin in the game. Larger attorney fees are ok with almost everyone vis-à-vis a large recovery, but no plaintiff wants to pay fees up front and then recover nothing.

There's a lot to include in a contingency fee contract. I'm happy to share mine for the asking. Just make sure you use a sliding scale fee that goes up if the case goes to trial. The client should have to consider increased risk and expenses just like we do when weighing a settlement proposal.

With flat fees sometimes you get what it's worth, and sometimes you might leave money on the table, but I'd rather have a flat fee up front than mess with billing. A good way to quote a flat fee is to visit with the potential clients enough to know, in your opinion, what legally needs to be done and your flat fee in advance if they want you to do it. Give them time to price you against your competition. Sometimes you'll be helping your competitors to underbid you, but that's ok; they'll regret it if you have bid fairly. For those who hire you, both sides will be satisfied with the agreement; for those who don't hire you, you'll have invested a little uncompensated time to be able to analyze the situation. That's what I do every day offering to send contingency contracts.

The importance of developing relationships with primary care doctors, both family practice medical doctors and chiropractic doctors, cannot be overstated.

Eventually, you want to develop a doctor referral list for the entire state or area where you practice. This should catalog primary care doctors and sub-specialty doctors listed by town or city.

On a local basis, the best way to get started is to ask your personal primary care doctor to assist. The relationships you develop with the primary care doctors will help your clients and will give you credibility when a client needs a doctor who will not charge money up front. Primary care doctors also can help with sub-specialty referrals when necessary.

62. DRESS

How should we dress in our office? One step above our clients. I don't mean to sound haughty; I am trying to communicate what our clients expect of us as they have communicated it to me and as I have studied the matter. For us to be parading around the office in dinner jackets would be just as offensive to a client as dressing down too much.

Even on a dress down Friday, during the heat of summer, or during a pandemic, we still must remember that clients will be in the office and that they will take offense if they are dressed up as much or more than we are. There are books on how to dress for success. Read the books.

In general, advise clients to dress for court the same way they would dress if they were going to their own church, in their "Sunday best." However, this general advice is often not enough. I have sometimes noticed that a particular garment or hairstyle worn to the office for a deposition gave the right impression and then suggested that the same thing be worn to court. I have arranged for a "professional" to assist in choosing the right attire for court. Usually someone who works in the office will have noticed and can help address potential problems.

Remind all that the judge wears a woolen robe to show respect for the law; the attorneys wear suits to show respect for the Court. Court is serious business.

Attorneys should always dress in business attire when going to court, even for a hearing.

Depositions and mediations are all business, yet dress is becoming more relaxed there. Just don't forget that with Zoom you're now more likely to be recorded.

Assuming no court appearances, I normally dress more formally on a Monday—you never know what's going to happen; then more casually for the rest of the week. I also keep a blazer and tie hanging in the office, just in case.

I once represented a businessman in a commission dispute. The lawsuit was driven by the real estate broker; the agent knew a commission wasn't owed. My client, who could buy Miami, and who probably has spent that much with the agent since, was cautioned on his dress for trial. "Don't worry. I understand." He showed up wearing a pair of shoes that had a huge hole in one of the soles and insisted on crossing his legs when testifying before the jury. I felt sorry for him before it was all over. So did the jury. We got a defense verdict. But I remind my defense colleagues it's easy to get a defense verdict. The burden of proof for a plaintiff isn't called a burden for nothing.

63. First Impressions

My first year out of law school a cousin was killed in a Jeep rollover. I was asked to represent the immediate family. The first thing I did was to seek out the best Jeep rollover attorney in the state to help me. At the time (1979) it was E. C. Gilbreath, who agreed to drive down from Fort Smith and meet with the family and me. I'll never forget the comment made by the in-law. "Well, he must be good, cause look at that car he just drove up in."

Don't kid yourself into thinking that, good or bad, first impressions don't matter.

I know this sounds shallow, and they perhaps would have hired E.C. had he hitchhiked in, but there was no doubt in my mind they were going to hire E.C., if he would have them.

Now for the other side of the coin before you start taking a limousine: When I go to court I take the trial truck.

My first real job was at a grocery store. The man who owned the store, on my first day of work, told me:

"If you can't find anything to do, sweep the floors. Here's a broom."

That's good advice for anyone at any job. Be a good worker. Improve the place. Anticipate. No job is too menial. Find something to do and do it well.

65. CANNED RESPONSES

If you're going to be in the law business you're going to answer some questions over and over again, and you're going to be called upon as a public speaker from time to time to deliver a prayer or a toast. Have some ready so you don't sound like a bumbling idiot.

Mark Twain admonished that a good impromptu speech requires much preparation. When asked by a prospective client whether they should invest in hiring an attorney I tell the story about how I had prepared my taxes myself for several years before becoming a lawyer and then had to make the decision whether to hire an accountant to prepare my taxes for me once things became complicated. Of course, I soon learned that what I paid the accountant was negligible compared to what the accountant saved me. I tell them I feel that lawyer fees work the same way.

When turning down a meritless case, many lawyers suggest another opinion. (I know, because many times the particularly crazy ones are told to call me). When turning down a medical negligence case that I sense probably would be unsuccessful I might suggest to the client who wants another opinion, "There are lots of young lawyers out there who will tell you that if you'll advance them a couple grand, they'll get the medical bills and hire a doctor to review them. Those lawyers are earnest; they'll spend the money getting the records and hiring a doctor, but, in my opinion, they'll eventually get to where you and I are right now. I would not recommend another opinion unless there are no up-front costs involved."

Don't wait until you need the money to seek a loan; then it's too late. In advance of need, negotiate credit lines. You might find it's easier to arrange several small credit lines with different banks than to convince one bank to supply all your borrowing needs. Both your trust account and your operating account will entice bankers to loan you money. Your profit sharing account gives you a relationship with another banker. Borrow money when you don't need it, and pay it back timely. Ask for increases in the credit lines when your income is up. Switch banks when you know they are too conservative for you.

Only attorneys should be authorized to sign checks and the fewer the better.

Bankers want a succession plan for your practice. They like to see credit lines utilized; and paid down to zero for at least 30 days at least once a year.

Bankers have rules and regulations they've got to tend. Help them out; have your account numbers ready when necessary. Send them current financial statements before they ask. When they need something from you to document their file, get it to them first thing. Let them know you're good for the money, hell or high water. Don't caveat a rising creek.

Bankers do not understand lavish spending when you owe money.

Don't burn bridges. The banking community is a small one. Bankers move around.

67. EMPOWER THE RECEPTIONIST

Have written procedures on how to answer your phones. Have directions to your office printed and handy at the reception desk. Have a log book at the front desk so that the receptionist knows where everyone is at all times. Take new calls personally. Communicate often with the receptionist, your first line of communication between you and those you seek to serve.

Discrimination cannot be tolerated. Realize the forwarding of offensive email can be deemed discrimination. What you consider offensive and what someone else considers offensive may not be the same. Generally, forwarding an email except for business purposes is ill advised.

Realize that personal comments such as "You're looking good … pretty … I like your hair, dress, etc.," can be offensive and are not appropriate in the work place.

I suggest adding to your policy and procedure manuals, "Any known discrimination should be reported to management immediately; a written report should be made with the allegations signed by the victim and witnesses."

69. Confirming the Statute of Limitations Date!

Why do we have a checklist item that requires us to confirm the date of incident and statute of limitations? Because missing a statute is the single largest cause of professional negligence for a law firm.

Don't take this duty lightly.

Err, if at all, on the conservative side.

Remember the date of death or the date of discovery of negligence may have nothing to do with the proper statute of limitations date.

When you do confirm the statute of limitations, make a note entry in the case management system explaining how and when you have done so.

Realize statutes of limitation assume a full year, not a year plus one day. E.g., if an Arkansas personal injury cause of action arose on January 31, 2021, the statute of limitations deadline to file suit will be January 30, 2024.

70. Traumatic Brain Injuries

Whenever someone loses consciousness they have, by definition of a traumatic brain injury, suffered a traumatic brain injury; and their case is probably worth at least policy limits. (One does not have to lose consciousness to suffer a TBI).

It's good for an attorney to have a basic understanding of TBI, because we have the luxury of spending more time with the client than a doctor has to spend with patients. Sometimes it's the attorney who alerts the doctor to a TBI.

Realize those who live with the client are better historians of the client's brain damage than the client is. Ask them questions about the client's memory loss, confusion, loss of balance, and frustration.

Ask the magic questions for determining whether someone suffered a loss of consciousness and, therefore, by most definitions, a TBI: "What's the last thing you remember before the crash? What's the first thing you remember after the crash?"

Realize the "blind spot" question is a good way to inquire about a traumatic brain injury, even over the phone. ("Look over your shoulder as though you are driving a car. Do you experience any dizziness or blurriness as you turn to focus behind you?")

Finally, if you or your client reasonably suspects a traumatic brain injury, realize that a neuropsychologist can do testing to document/prove the severity of the traumatic brain injury. A life care planner can project the future costs associated with properly dealing with the TBI, a vocational rehabilitation expert can opine as to how the TBI will affect the client's earning capacity, and an economist can project the cost of all the necessary care and income loss.

With the advancement of digital technology there is a lot more information that needs to be understood to handle a traumatic brain injury case, but the above will help you get started.

Before the advent of the public defender offices, criminal cases were the bread and butter of a consumer practice. Not all consumer lawyers handled criminal cases, but most did.

If you have not yet handled a criminal law case, do not be afraid to do so. Criminal law defense is straight forward. At the risk of over-simplification, you start by reading the statute the client is alleged to have violated and then set out to distinguish the client's facts from the statute, using the criminal law procedure statutes and case law in the process. I urge you to take criminal cases, at least early in your career. I guarantee it'll make you a better lawyer.

Remember that delay works to the benefit of the defendant; that it's probably malpractice to allow a Defendant to give a statement in a criminal case.

My first criminal jury trial occurred my first year out of law school. While in law school I had worked as a deputy public defender. In that job I'd made contacts with the police, prosecutors, and other court personnel, so referrals came my way as soon as I'd hung my shingle.

My client, Don, was charged with 7 counts of aggravated robbery, all performed during the course of a few days, all of the victims' establishments with security cameras. Don's disguise was a single pane dive mask which highlighted his big baby blues when he looked up at the camera. His weapon was a big curved-end butcher knife.

Don came from a very good family who could not believe he would do such things. And they insisted on a trial to prove his innocence.

I knew my work was cut out for me. While Don came from a loving family, he was not a sympathetic figure. I sought out an expert witness who could help me unravel the mens rea, the intent that was needed on top of the damning photographs.

I'd heard of a particular forensic psychologist that did not mind helping criminal defendants. His testimony ended with, "During those robberies Don was of such a state of intoxication that it was like a 5 year old boy picking a shiny dime up off the floor. He did not know he was doing anything wrong."

A few days earlier I'd been walking up the steps of the court-house when a wino stopped my stride. "Hey man. Do you need a witness?" I smiled, and he laughed.

During closing argument I told the story of my Uncle Stewart, who was a pitiful drunk, harmless as long as he didn't drive, who would shake and cry inconsolably when he drank. He would never intentionally hurt anyone. It drew an objection, but the judge wanted to hear the story, or maybe just figured the bumbling first year lawyer was harmless.

I had bet that every family has an Uncle Stewart. Two older ladies on the jury refused to convict.

At 11 p.m. The prosecutor walked up to me. "I'm going to make your client an offer, but first I want you to know what I'm gonna do if the offer is rejected. I'm gonna re-file each of these cases, one at a time, and go for the max each time. You can't do this 7 times in a row. He'll serve at least 50 years, probably 350. I'll do everything in my power to make sure the sentences run con-secutively. Or he can plead all cases to five years. Visit with your client. The offer is rescinded if the judge declares a mistrial."

Back then, maybe even today, the minimum plea deal for aggravated robbery was 7 years, for one charge. I knew that. Don knew that. Don made the decision. He figured to be out in two years.

I had to remind myself that Don was the client when, just before midnight, he and I strode to the podium to enter a guilty plea. In the gallery, his mother gasped. The two ladies on the jury stared at me in disbelief, their eyes seeking understanding. Don thanked me.

It wasn't too many weeks after that I received a call from Don's sister, rather late at night. "Hi, Jean. Good to hear from you."

"This is not a pleasant call, Gary. I just wanted you to know that Don was raped tonight. And it's all your fault."

A few months later I was interviewing an imprisoned witness. As I was being escorted through the general population of the prison I saw Don, a trusty by then, broom and rolling trash can in hand, smiling, nodding, waving at me, across the sea of forms and faces. We didn't get to speak, but I could tell he held me no ill will.

When the sister had called I had shuddered. Sympathized. I'd felt horrible for him, at the situation. I had nightmares, repeating in my head all that had happened. But no matter how I replayed it, it hurt, and I couldn't do anything about it. Nor would I have done anything differently if I had had to do it again.

72. How to Explain Why a Trial Lawyer Will Represent Someone Who Is Negligent or Charged with a Crime

Everyone is innocent until proven guilty; the prosecutor has the burden of proof and it's my job to make sure the prosecutor meets that burden. All of that can be achieved, and the defendant doesn't have to testify. I would not knowingly put a client on the stand and allow the client to tell a lie.

Civil defense attorneys sometimes have to explain how they can represent someone who obviously was at fault. They are honoring the adversarial system. It is the plaintiff's duty to prove negligence, proximate cause, and damages.

Negotiating with an insurance company is like negotiating with dad:

"May I have 5 dollars?"

"What are you going to do with 3 dollars?"

"Won't you have enough with 2 dollars?"

"Here's a dollar."

Part of getting a good deal is knowing when to make a demand/offer.

Never let your client appear desperate.

Being shrewd isn't necessarily being a good negotiator.

It's elementary, but if you have to be the first to make an offer, go high.

Set a deadline.

Debts that have been owed for a long time are often cleared for a song just to get them off the books.

Cases settle at the end of the year, at Christmas, sometimes to get them off the reserves of the insurance company and sometimes because money is needed for Christmas presents or essentials.

Cases sometimes settle when you're finally pitted against the reasonable opponent, or the opponent with a soul.

While most negotiators fear the contract rule that a counter offer is a rejection of an offer and don't want to risk the offer going away, that has never yet negatively affected my clients. My experience is that once an offer has been made by an insurance company or defense attorney, they usually will continue to honor their original offer for a reasonable time, even after a counter.

74. Some Employment
Interview Questions

At what age did you first get a driver's license or permit? (I find the ones who get the permit as soon as possible to be self-starters).

On a 1-10 scale tell me how organized you are.

I use the old "psychological test" probably found now on the internet. You are walking on an outdoor trail. Describe the trail. (Looking for references to color and light, which, presumably, tells how happy somebody is). I leave out the one about water. You come across a snake on the trail. What do you do? (I'm looking for someone who doesn't turn around and run).

Why do you want this job?

If you could have one book what would it be?

If you could have one gun what would it be?

Where do you hope to be 10 years from now?

When I make a job offer to an attorney my hope is they will work here forever, but stuff happens. On the day our paths fork, I probably will ask you to continue some of the representations entrusted to you because that would be in the best interest of the clients. However, I need to know you and I will not be litigating over the others. Do I have your commitment to honor the employment contracts that the firm has with any of the clients entrusted to you?

What is the default place you keep your home key?

How do you spell supercalifragilisticexpialidocious?

75. RESIST SARCASM, EMBRACE PROFESSIONALISM

It was a heated trial. Most of them are. Opposing counsel had the floor, cross examining a witness we had just called. A siren got louder and louder, and eventually went right past the courthouse. "Gary, that must be for one of your potential clients. Need to go?"

I ignored defense counsel, but the jury did not. I could tell in their eyes when he said it they were horrified. I could tell it wasn't my lawyering but his that had driven the million dollar verdict.

Did I mention to treat opposing counsel as though they don't exist?

76. WHERE I'M HEADED THESE DAYS

The wheelhouse is professional negligence (medical and legal), catastrophic injuries, and mass torts.

The particular mass torts we handle change from time to time, but we usually can help, even when it's to advise against getting involved for whatever reason. As of this writing our primary focus is on Catholic Church sexual abuse, Zantac, RoundUp, and talcum powder which has caused ovarian cancer.

We are looking to refer things that do not fit into that wheelhouse.

For any complex case consider a timeline.

We include "Prepare timeline of events" as a checklist prompt in our case management system.

By the way, I've not mentioned case management software because I figure everyone's using something by now. If not, do.

Just because this topic is very short does not mean it's not very important.

Set a deadline if you want something to happen.

Focus on things that have a time deadline.

Put your own time deadline on things that need focus.

Two of the most important things successful lawyers do is set and heed deadlines.

Answer questions regarding timing, (when will x happen) in terms of days, weeks, months, or years. Sometimes the best you can promise is twenty-first century. Err on the conservative side to help manage expectations.

"When can I get my check?"

Well, of course that depends upon when we receive the check from the insurance company; that should be days or weeks, the settlement agreement calls for 15 days, but sometimes things drag out. I have an ethical obligation to let you know when I receive funds on your behalf, so receipt of the check can be projected in the next few weeks. What's harder to predict is when we can get liens on your case reduced, waived, or defeated. If we're talking about private lienholders, that should be weeks, not months; but if we're talking about Medicaid or Medicare, that will take months, at least.

80. Medical Negligence Primer

Again, discipline yourself to use the term medical negligence, not medical malpractice. All a plaintiff has to prove is negligence, not intentional conduct. Malpractice has the connotation of intentional conduct.

There are good reasons most attorneys elect not to handle medical negligence cases. The odds of success are not good. Even when on the front end the cause of action sounds to be meritorious, more often than not, after having spent lots of money and time developing the case, we learn it is not meritorious.

Even the meritorious claims do not settle—at least not until on the courthouse steps, after you've hired numerous expert witnesses and gotten past the motion for summary judgment.

The medical negligence statutes lobbied for by the medical communities, greatly favor the doctors, nurses, and hospitals. Generally, the medical community enjoys a two year statute of limitations, while for the rest of us who harm someone negligently, the statute of limitations is three years. The medical industrial complex is powerful.

Doctors and nurses are well educated, communicate well, and are put on a pedestal in our society. The Plaintiff's expert witnesses, required under the medical negligence statute to make a prima facie case, usually hail from out of state because local doctors and nurses won't testify against each other. Bringing doctors in from out of state, paying their hourly rates from portal to portal, is extremely expensive. We have spent as much as $321,000.00 prosecuting a single medical negligence case. Case selection is key.

Statistically, most medical negligence cases get dismissed before trial; of those that make it to trial the majority result in a defense verdict; when the Plaintiff does achieve a verdict, an appeal usually is filed.

If you accept a case, you get the records. It is OK to accept the case, get the contract signed, get the records, and then close if no case. Just keep in mind during the interim you are at risk because there are no records with which to verify the statute of limitations.

As a general rule, do not tell a caller that you will review the records if the caller will supply them. This sets up an unacceptable situation where you have a duty, but maybe no contract; and maybe, for a long time, no records to review. Even if you have a contract, you do not want to be at the mercy of the client getting the records. During that waiting time you have a liability and need to be aggressively prosecuting the case.

Do not encourage a client who already has the records to expect a review during the original client interview. Usually, if a file already exists, it is better to have a chance to review it before the meeting with the client.

Beware of:

1. Diabetes cases. Good people with diabetes often get bad results, making causation difficult if not impossible to prove.

2. Infection cases in general. Infections are a known risk of any surgery. To win an infection case, concentrate on failure to diagnose and negligent management once known.

3. Dental malpractice cases. The reasoning here is based on damages—most dental malpractice cases do not have damages sufficient to warrant the expense and risk of prosecution.

4. Orthopedic/podiatry cases where the patient is not satisfied with the result, e.g., a broken arm that was set and,

after healing, is obviously crooked. Causation might have been the original injury. Special damages probably won't be as much as litigation costs. Beware of multiple back surgeries, or orthopedic surgeries to treat trauma.

5. Someone wanting to sue over an elective cosmetic surgery result. Chances are one of those legs of the three legged milk stool is going to get knocked out from under you.

6. Cases where the statute of limitations does not allow sufficient time to do an adequate investigation. This sounds obvious, but it's even more important in medical negligence cases.

7. Cases already filed by another lawyer who has decided to exit the case for whatever reason. At a minimum, understand the reasons for exiting and confirm service of process has been perfected timely.

8. The potential client who does not call on a lawyer until after receiving a high medical bill.

9. Heart attack cases.

10. Prior smokers or current smokers—they tend not to heal as well as non-smokers, thus a causation issue.

11. Failure to diagnose or failure to administer TPA in stroke cases unless an imaging baseline was established that allows for measurement of the delay.

12. Informed consent cases—it's a swearing match, and 50/50 ties go in favor of the Defendant.

13. Inadequate care in prison cases.

14. Failed cataract surgery cases.

15. Failed penile prosthesis cases.

16. Contaminated blood cases.

17. Multiple defendant cases because of the additional complexity and costs, including the possibility of overlapping venues—when the suit must be filed in the county where the negligence occurred and more than one medical provider from more than one jurisdiction contributed to the problem.

18. Clear negligence/causation/but low damages cases. Low damages don't warrant the cost or risk of litigation. Sometimes they settle, but find out early on. Usually, damages must be significant, bordering on catastrophic.

19. General rules. Some of our biggest recoveries have been for diabetics, for clients with infections, for clients who had been turned down by other attorneys.

"$5 million. Amount that a Maine dairy company will pay its drivers after a judge ruled that the lack of one Oxford comma in a list of tasks legally exempt from overtime pay meant their work isn't covered by the law."

Use the Oxford comma.

For want of a comma, a 5 million dollar ruling was lost for vagueness.

I enjoy subtle jokes, Oxford commas and irony.

The late John Walker was a mentor. During my year as president of the Southern Trial Lawyers he received the War Horse Award, becoming the fourth Arkansan, following the late Walter Niblock, Hon. William R. Wilson, and the late Hon. Henry Woods, to be so honored.

On my first day in Judge Holt's Little Rock Municipal Court I was trying a hot check case as a Rule XII deputy public defender. I had been appointed ten minutes before the trial. John Walker noticed I could use some help. With no introduction other than a smile he suggested I ask the state's witness whether my client had asked if the check could be postdated. She said yes. "Now move for dismissal, because in America one cannot be imprisoned for a debt."

I won one of my first cases, thanks to John Walker. (The sentence for another defendant I was appointed to represent that day was to, "Get out of town by sundown").

With checks having become anachronistic I almost didn't include this story, but some of you might appreciate the moral: It never hurts to postdate a check.

83. Legal Malpractice

How to turn a mediocre case into a multi-million dollar case? Miss a deadline.

If you or someone you supervise commits malpractice, settle the case; or turn it over to your carrier and do as they suggest.

Not every act of professional negligence has a remedy. The "case within a case" defense (causation) is sometimes tough to overcome. Lawyers are difficult adversaries—they know the law and all the defenses and delays available to them. However, there are many times when a lawyer has made a mistake and readily admits it. There still remains the question: What is the cost/value of that mistake?

Try your good cases. Settle the rest. It seems counter intuitive, but you don't want to be trying the bad ones. Make them pay full value for the good ones.

85. SHOULD I GIVE A WRITTEN STATEMENT TO THE ADJUSTER?

I was taught in law school never to give a written statement pre-litigation. Everyone knows the more prior statements there are the more chances of finding an inconsistent one for cross exam.

And most trial attorneys will tell you the same.

But the reality is that some smaller cases will settle if the adjuster can mark off her/his list, "Statement from Claimant."

So, if I know suit will be filed, no statement. But otherwise, on the smaller claims especially, it's okay to allow a statement either in person, over the phone, or even on written questions.

86. Referrals—Why Pay an Attorney Who Refers You Someone?

Do a good job on every case, and especially do a good job on every case referred to you from someone in your profession.

Accept referrals. Send referrals. Never forget those who referred to you.

1. Know the cost of procuring the intake and conversion to a contract.

2. Know the referring attorney provides continued value in multiple ways, e.g., continuing client communications and local lawyer presence and knowledge.

3. It doesn't matter to me if I make less by bringing in a friend to help prosecute a case and share the fee. The client is better served because it brings more attention, knowledge, and experience at no extra cost to the client.

Do you have to disclose to the client that association and fee split? Of course, it's a parenthetical paragraph that goes right in the attorney client contract:

> Additional associate counsel may be employed by said Law Firm, but such association shall not increase the total attorneys' fee as provided for herein. Further, all attorneys as named above will be sharing in a division of the contingent fee as set out above, and they agree to assume the same legal responsibility to the Client for the performance of the services in question as if the attorney or law firm were a partner of the other attorneys or firms involved.

The fee shall be divided _____% to Law Offices of Gary Green, P.A., and ___% to

_____.

Expenses shall be advanced _____% by Law Offices of Gary Green, P.A. and _____% by

_____.

I started law school fresh out of college and started practicing law when I was 26 years old. I'm now of retirement age. I've been paying association fees all that time (I believe pursuant to Rule 1.5), and I've never had it come up as an issue that I had paid an association fee unethically or against the attorney disciplinary rules.

Be more than fair with your referral attorneys and with your clients. That's why we have the policy of not keeping a fee of more than the client receives. Sometimes there's just not enough room for a full fee. Same thing goes with referral attorneys—if they entrust something to you that goes unexpectedly send them half of whatever fee you receive, despite your agreement with them for less. For example, our standard fee split with a referring attorney is 1/3 to the referring attorney whether requested or not for the work already done and for the client communications and local boots on the ground appearances to be done in the future. If we unexpectedly have to bring in other attorneys or incur extraordinary expenses, we share whatever net fee we receive 50/50 with the referring attorney.

When you have to round something off, give the extra penny to the other person.

A long, long, time ago, during my law school years, I accompanied my grandfather to visit his lawyer. My grandfather didn't have much, but he wanted everything properly tended. We sat in a reception area dominated by book shelves.

"Have you read all these books?" He smiled. We both smiled. We both knew the answer to most questions was somewhere if we just worked hard enough to find it. And that was before Google.

Might we need to rethink lawyer education and licensing? It seems today anybody with a brain and a computer can find a statute, case law, and commentary. Briefs don't even need abstracting anymore.

Isn't "thinking like a lawyer" just deductive reasoning? We probably should rethink law school, at least shorten the three years it takes and reduce cost by concentrating on basics and eliminating fluff. The internet has democratized education.

I have found a quick draw agreement to be invaluable in resolving many kinds of partnership, shareholder, or buy/sell disputes. It's fair and efficient. Any one at any time can set the price. But it must be a price at which they're willing either to buy or sell. Below is my standard form.

> In the event any shareholder (optionor for purposes of this provision), at any time, wishes to buy or sell, pledge, transfer or otherwise dispose of such shares as he may own, he must give written notice to his fellow shareholders. Such notice must contain the price at which he is willing to buy or sell.
>
> Fellow shareholders (optionees) have ten (10) days to respond from date of receipt of the above written notice as to their desire to sell their shares at the price set by the optionor, or to buy the optionor's shares at the price set. Such response shall be written. Failure to respond by the end of this ten day period is an election by the optionee to sell to the optionor. The Sale shall be completed within thirty (30) days of the end of the ten (10) day period referenced above.
>
> If the optionee elects to sell, then such sale shall be completed within thirty (30) days of the end of the ten (10) day period referenced above. If the optionee has, by the end of the ten day period, notified the optionor that he is purchasing the optionor's stock, then the optionee shall have sixty (60) days from the end of the ten (10) day period to close the transaction. All purchases or sales are for cash.

Should more than one optionee desire to buy the optionor's stock, optionees shall purchase such stock on a pro rata basis according to such shares as they hold before the exercise of the quick-draw provisions. Thus, if A, B, C, and D own 25 shares each and A acts as optionor by setting a price of $10.00 per share then, if only B and C wish to buy, B and C each get to purchase one-half of A's stock or 12.5 shares each. Should only one optionee decide to purchase under this provision then he shall buy all such shares offered.

This provision is separate from and in addition to the right of first refusal and may be invoked at any time (including simultaneously with a right of first refusal option) by any shareholder. All purchases or sales are for cash.

Any one at any time can set the price. But it must be a price at which they're willing either to buy or sell.

89. Font and Salutations

If you don't understand this already, you will soon enough. Judges do not like small fonts. We use Arial.

Business letters sign off with "Very truly yours," "Truly yours," or "Truly," but letters to a judge should be signed, "Respectfully submitted."

Everyone knows we can't see microbes and, therefore, proving liability in food poisoning cases is dicey.

Sometimes you might get lucky if you inspect the health department complaints against a suspected defendant.

We once represented half a bus of school children, the half who ate chicken. The other half who had a hamburger were fine.

Think positively. Choose to be happy.

Your cup is either half full or half empty. You choose.

Even though your cup is half full, when your fuel tank is half empty, it's time to think about filling it.

Don't buy gas at night.

Don't ever set anything on top of a vehicle.

Be positive. Be happy.

I thought surely I could get through this book politically cor-
rectly. Less than horrific scars to a male, per adjusters and juries,
build character; scars to a female are highly compensable. If you're
lucky you'll be dealing with a female adjuster. Deselect your jury
in favor of women.

Find and invest in that place your mind can be free from everything, where you practice your arguments, think up your themes, and find your focus. Some can do it anywhere with a mantra. I do it better outside when I'm tending the mundane, like right now as I'm pruning muscadines writing this sentence on my phone.

I suggest you have a little hobby/business on the side just so you know how hard it is to make a living in a business. Practicing law is a piece of cake compared to what our clients have to do.

95. Underinsured and Uninsured Motorist Coverage

The *Arkansas Democrat-Gazette* has reported that every fifth driver on the road is uninsured. My experience is that most who have insurance at all are underinsured. Minimum liability limits in Arkansas are $25,000. Most surrounding states have similar low minimums. When we tell our legislators that $25,000 is woefully inadequate for serious injuries, they respond, "That's what underinsured motorist coverage is for." They're right, of course. But most people don't know till it's too late. I recommend a "check-up" with your insurance agent. UM (uninsured) and UIM (underinsured) coverages are a bargain and allow you to insure yourself against bad actors.

Do not forget, our legislature and courts deem UM and UIM coverage so important that, unless our clients waive them in writing, the coverage is presumed by law.

Realize that a UM or UIM claim is a direct action against the insurance company based upon your contract with it. If payments are not made to you promptly, you can add the 12% statutory penalty and, potentially, attorney fees to the claim.

Before accepting a policy limits offer from the liability carrier, you must give written notice to the UIM carrier. This gives the UIM carrier time to run an asset check on the underinsured motorist to make sure there are no additional avenues of recovery. If the UIM carrier objects within 30 days from the date of the written notice of the proposed settlement with the liability carrier, to protect its subrogation right, the UIM carrier must make payment to its insured in an amount equal to the proposed settlement amount agreed to by the liability carrier.

It has been my experience that the UIM carrier usually does not object to the liability settlement, and gives consent prior to the 30 day deadline, and, therefore, waives subrogation.

A copy of our standard form statutory notice to the UIM carrier follows:

3/30/21

CERTIFIED MAIL ARTICLE NO:
RETURN RECEIPT REQUESTED

Re: Our client:
Your insured:
Date of loss:
Claim number:

Dear :

In compliance with Arkansas Code Annotated § 23-89-209, please be advised on behalf of we have received a settlement offer from in the amount of $ representing the total amount of coverage available to for damages incurred. Policy limits are per incident.

Accordingly, in conjunction with my prior correspondence to your office on activating underinsured provisions with your company, a written summary of pecuniary losses incurred, including copies of all medical bills, is enclosed for your review.

Also enclosed herewith you will find the following:

1. Written authorization or a court order authorizing the underinsured motorist insurer to obtain medical reports from all employers and medical providers; and

2. Written confirmation from the tortfeasor's liability insurer as to the amount of the alleged tortfeasor's liability limits and the terms of the tentative settlement.

Very truly yours,

Enclosures: summary, copies of all medical bills, medical release, confirmation of liability limits.

Beware Super Duper designations. They might just be Who's Who for lawyers. And if you've been practicing long enough to have established a good reputation that isn't yet recognized by Martindale Hubble, contact it and request a re-do. Mention it might be fairer if some of your out-of-state attorney friends serve as your references.

Get down low for high wind. Go to higher ground if flooding. Who's got time to think emergently? Have a creed. Follow it all the time, especially during emergencies. Think of it when you can't think of anything else. Ours is:

> LAW OFFICES OF GARY GREEN represents people. We offer prompt, quality, and convenient legal services at a fair price. We strive to improve the communities in which we live, to better the lives of those with whom we interact, and to teach and help those who need our services to find justice, equality, and respect. We consider it an honor to be called upon for representation.

98. Consistent Persistent Giving

Choose a charity and establish a relationship. Put together a plan for persistent giving. Involve everyone in your office so that they know what triggers a gift and are empowered to make it happen. Make the contributions manageable so that you won't be tempted to skip them. Ours is Mothers Against Drunk Driving, MADD. One of our slogans is, "This law firm makes a contribution to MADD in honor of every victim we represent against a drunk driver." This plan has allowed us to donate almost $100,000 to MADD over the years.

99. ADOPTION

Standing with a client who has just won a jury trial is a good feeling, but it pales to standing with a family who has just finished the challenging and tense process of adopting a child.

Everyone in the courtroom is happy.

Some don't realize how the adversarial process has played out. If still alive, biological mom was probably represented by a different attorney. She and her attorney previously have consented to the final hearing and have approved the decree. As in all cases involving children the rule that was considered was, "What is in the child's best interest?" That rule was considered by biological mom or others acting in her stead even before the judge came to the same conclusion.

If you get the chance to ethically help someone with an adoption that is in the best interest of the child, I strongly recommend you do it, despite your usual wheelhouse.

163

Justice doesn't just happen to good people.
Justice is earned by being worthy of justice.
Justice is earned by pushing for it.
Justice is earned by demanding it. Making it happen.
The right to justice is protected by our 7th Amendment.
Our right to redress a wrong is based on the adversarial system.
Expect your personal life to be examined.
Expect to be aggressively cross examined.
Expect every truth you assert to be challenged.
Justice has to be earned.

101. MEDICARE/MEDICAID LIEN RESOLUTION INSTRUCTIONS

Lien resolution, particularly Medicare/Medicaid, has become the bane of the trial lawyer's existence. I hope this helps.

MEDICARE

1. Be sure to use ONLY the contact information listed below:
    MSPRC-NGHP
    P.O. Box 138832
    Oklahoma City, OK 73113
    FAX: 1-405-869-3309

2. Send letter to Medicare/caid. See attached example.

3. Fax letter to Medicare with a copy of the contract and signed medical authorization. If it is a medical negligence case and suit has been filed, you must include a copy of the Complaint. This is only for medical negligence cases.

4. The first response letter you will receive will be the Rights and Responsibilities letter.

5. The second letter you will receive is the Conditional Payment Letter (CPL). You will need to review the claims listed to make sure they are related. As a general rule, Medicare will list all claims filed during the requested time frame even if they are unrelated. In order to confirm claims

are related, you will need to check the ICD 10 Codes. You can do this at: https://www.icd10data.com/.

DO NOT REQUEST FINAL LIEN/DEMAND LETTER UNTIL ALL DISPUTES ARE COMPLETED.

6.   Disputes: Disputes are submitted via fax at 1-405-869-3309. List each item that is not related and state the reason why. This process will be repeated each time an updated CPL is received.

7.   Settlement. Once a case settles, the following information should be faxed to Medicare 1-405-869-3309:
   1.   Amount of settlement;
   2.   Amount of Attorney's Fees;
   3.   Case Expenses;
   4.   Date of settlement;
   5.   Copy of final settlement breakdown (unsigned as we do not yet have Medicare demand amount).

NOTES: Only report amount of Med-Pay if funds are NOT paid to the providers. This step must be completed even if NO payments were made.

The best way to submit is to use the form provided by Medicare with the CPL.

A letter containing the same information will also work.

8.   The final letter you will receive is the Demand Letter. This is the total amount owed after Medicare has calculated the procurement cost reduction.

MEDICAID:

Please note these instructions are specific to Arkansas Medicaid. While most other states operate in a similar manner, procedures may be slightly different.

1. Be sure to use ONLY the contact information listed below:
   Medicaid
   Arkansas Dept. of Human Services
   Third Party Liability Section
   P.O. Box 1437, Slot S296
   Little Rock, AR 72203
   FAX: 501-682-1644

2. Send letter to Medicare/caid. See attached example.

3. Fax SFL to Medicaid with a copy of the signed medical authorization. No additional documentation is required.

4. You will receive a response from either Medicaid or HMS. The response will come from HMS 95% of the time.

HMS—AR Dept. of Human Services Division of Medical Services
Third Party Liability Unit
5615 Highpoint Drive, Suite 100
Irving, TX 75038

5. Nine times out of 10, you will not receive the payment log with the first response letter. As soon as the payment log is received, you will need to review the claims listed to make sure they are related. As a general rule, Medicaid will list all

claims filed during the requested time frame even if they are unrelated. In order to confirm claims are related, you will need to check the ICD 10 Codes if the description is not listed on the payment log. You can do this at: https://www.icd10data.com/ . HMS will normally list both the ICD10 Code and description.

Disputes: Disputes are submitted via fax at 1-844-845-8353. List each item that is not related and state the reason why:

LAW OFFICES OF GARY GREEN, P.A.

1001 La Harpe Boulevard
Little Rock, Arkansas 72201
501-224-7400
Fax 501-224-2294
email: ggreen@gGreen.com
www.gGreen.com

December 27, 2018

VIA TELEFAX NO. 1-844-845-8353

Claims Adjuster
HMS - AR Dept of Human Serv - Div of Med Serv.
Third Party Liability Unit
5615 Highpoint Drive, Suite 100
Irving, TX 75038

Re: Our client   :   Jane Doe
     Your insured :   Jane Doe
     Date of loss :   6/1/2018
     Claim number :   801116

Dear Claims Adjuster:

Ms. Doe was involved in two separate motor vehicle collisions. The first was on June 1, 2018. The second was on August 1, 2018. The HMS case number for the August 1, 2018 collision is 178117. Medicaid was reimbursed in full for case number 178117 on December 1, 2018. A copy of the transmittal letter is attached hereto and labeled as Exhibit "A". A copy of the final lien for case number 178117 is attached hereto and labeled as Exhibit "B".

There are four items listed on the final lien for case number 801116 that have already been reimbursed under case number 178117:

8/1/18:	Radiology Associates	$250.00
8/1/18:	Saline Hospital, LLC	$150.00
8/1/18:	Medical Emergency Trauma Assoc.	$85.00
8/2/18:	Kroger Limited Partnership I	$25.00

A copy of the final lien for case number 801116 showing the duplicate listings is attached hereto and labeled as Exhibit "C".

Please forward an updated/corrected final lien for case number 801116. The case settled today. Ms. Doe's last date of treatment for case number 801116 was July 10, 2018.

Thank you.

Very truly yours,

Tara M. Ashton
Claims Manager
tara.ashton@gGreen.com
Extension 3025

/ek

Enclosures

PRINTED WITH SOY INK

168

This process will be repeated each time an updated payment log is received.

6. Settlement. Once the case settles, the following information should be faxed to HMS at 1-844-845-8353:
   1. Date of Settlement;
   2. Last date of related treatment;
   3. Request for final lien amount.

LAW OFFICES OF GARY GREEN, P.A.

1001 La Harpe Boulevard
Little Rock, Arkansas 72201
501-224-7400
Fax 501-224-2294
email: ggreen@gGreen.com
www.gGreen.com

February 26, 2020

VIA TELEFAX NO. 1-844-845-8353

Ms. Eva Hasty
HMS - AR Dept of Human Serv - Div of Med Serv.
Third Party Liability Unit
5615 Highpoint Drive, Suite 100
Irving, TX 75038

Re: Our client   :   Jane Doe
     Your insured :   Jane Doe
     Date of loss   :   10/1/2018
     Claim number: 701119

Dear Ms. Hasty:

The above referenced case settled today. Ms. Doe's last day of related medical treatment was January 2, 2019.

Please forward your final lien amount.

Thank you.

Very truly yours,

Tara M. Ashton
Claims Manager
tara.ashton@gGreen.com
Extension 3025
Direct Fax: 501-325-1598

/ek

7. The turnaround time to receive a final lien from HMS is 30 days. **If you re-request the final lien before the 30 days has expired, it will delay processing!**

The power to file a lawsuit is an awesome power, not to be taken lightly or abused.

Never accept someone's business card without giving one of your own in return.

Take time to plan, to become inspired, and then to implement.

Use a small recorder in the car. Record ideas and then implement.

It's easier to get up early than it is to rush in the morning. To get the sleep you need, get it by going to bed earlier, rather than trying to sleep till the last possible minute. If you normally take two hours to do the things you like to do in the morning, get up at whatever time it takes to accomplish that.

Set up a system for regular ethical bonuses based on production—that accomplishes motivation and fairness. You can always top that off with discretionary bonuses, but even when you can't give a discretionary bonus, the salary and reliable bonus should adequately compensate.

The key to happiness is to always be planning a vacation.

Don't call the adjuster or opposing counsel on Monday when trying to resolve a case. You'll get a better result any other day.

Remember to relax. Find and foster that place where a blanket of calm descends upon your soul.

Put in another room screens that light up in the middle of the night; silence all those unimportant notices.

Review tomorrow's calendar today!

When it's dark and raining and the bullets are flying, you don't want to be worried about where the door is.

Be aware that, legally, only U.S. Citizens or green card holders can apply for a Social Security number. Those without a social security number still can file claims in court. (We file a motion in limine to preclude mention of nationality, which would not be relevant and could be prejudicial).

You can delegate more than you can do yourself.

Delegate work. Don't delegate thinking or responsibility.

Keep an electronic paper trail.

Backup the backup. Have a system. Have three people responsible. Put the final backup in your possession, preferably daily, at least weekly.

Keep your pump primed, your home fires burning, and your wires wound up.

Find something to make, grow, or sell.

Schedule the office cleaning person or crew during office hours, mainly because if your staff sees the work while it's being done, you'll receive fewer complaints. It's also one less security key you've got to have outstanding.

Embrace the negatives. Be preemptive.

Law and politics are adversarial processes.

Don't burn your non-suit get out of jail card unless you have to. You or the next lawyer might need it. Beware the right to voluntarily dismiss and then re-file within a year isn't recognized in all states.

Do charge family and friends something. Reduce your normal fee—they will appreciate the reduction and feel they can "complain," if something isn't right.

What's the hardest thing about being a lawyer? The hardest thing about law school was three more years of study while friends were out celebrating life. Still, it's the time commitment. Indeed, Rumpole, the law is a jealous mistress.

That's it. If you're with me this far, there's one more thing I want to discuss with you. Write your own paper chase compendium. Start right now by making a working title, paper file. Now you've taken the first step. If you want to accelerate things, tell someone what you've done. But, if you're like me, you'll want to be a little more relaxed about it. Throw into that file stuff that will someday go into your book. Be descriptive. Don't be too brief. You don't want to pull out forty years from now, "Three ducks walked into a bar…" and expect to remember the point you thought was important at the time.

Eventually, make an outline.

Write the first sentence.

Ideally, write the ending and work from there.

There's no hurry. You'll get around to it when you want to. You'll know when it's time.

Feel free to expound on stuff I have merely highlighted; to include stuff I forgot to mention.

Don't worry about originality. Everything I learned from others. Even when I thought I might have had an original idea or two, verification was a problem.

You'll have fun doing it, at reminiscing.

Everybody has at least one good book in them.

I challenge you to do it!

And I hope you'll remember to send me a copy.

In his spare time, Gary Green enjoys wordsmithing, gardening, and growing the grapes for, fermenting, and bottling Champagnezee.

www.ingramcontent.com/pod-product-compliance
Lightning Source LLC
Chambersburg PA
CBHW050500190326
41458CB00005B/1369